AN ILLUMINATING
EXPERIENCE
IN THE **WORD**

praying
ephesians

CHRISTIN DITCHFIELD

WORTHY
PUBLISHING

Published by Worthy Publishing, a division of Worthy Media, Inc., 134 Franklin Road, Suite 200, Brentwood, Tennessee 37027.

HELPING PEOPLE EXPERIENCE THE HEART OF GOD

eBook available at www.worthypublishing.com

Audio distributed through Oasis Audio; visit www.oasisaudio.com

Library of Congress Control Number: 2012940557

For foreign and subsidiary rights, contact Riggins International Rights Services, Inc.; www.rigginsrights.com

ISBN: 978-1-936034-95-6 (hardcover)

Cover Design: Andy Meyer, Grey Matter Group
Cover Images: shield – © Getty Images, photographed by "Magictorch" (Image #92418481) http://magictorch.com; sky – © Veer, photographed by Mazzachi (Image #3336785)
Interior Design and Typesetting: Kimberly Sagmiller, FudgeCreative.com

Printed in the United States of America
12 13 14 15 16 17 RRD 8 7 6 5 4 3 2 1

CONTENTS

INTRODUCTION

❝ For he chose us in him before the creation of the world to be holy and blameless in his sight. ❞

—Ephesians 1:4

Before time began, God chose us to be His children. He deliberately decided to create each and every one of us to be uniquely His. He welcomed us into His family and made us a part of His family tree. As God's children, we have been given an incredible legacy—a fabulous heritage—an amazing inheritance!

"His divine power has given us everything we need for a godly life through our knowledge of him who called us by his own glory and goodness" (2 Peter 1:3). God has given us everything we need to live a life of love and joy and peace. A life of hope. A life of faith. A life of discipline and self-control. A life of balance—physically, emotionally, mentally, and spiritually. A life of courage and strength and victory! We can live strong, because we've been chosen for a life of greatness.

Yet too often we live instead a life of emptiness, weakness, frustration, discouragement, defeat, and despair. We live in a state of spiritual starvation and poverty, when we are children of the King!

The book of Ephesians, unlike most of the other letters in the New Testament, wasn't written to combat error or expose false teachings or to clear up problems in the local church. The apostle Paul wrote simply to encourage the believers in Ephesus to live strong. He wanted to teach them about the life Jesus has called us to and what it means to live for Him.

During the next fifty-two devotional experiences, we'll pray through Ephesians. We'll allow the Holy Spirit to speak into our hearts and over our lives the Word that God has spoken to us. We'll ask Him to do in us and through us all that He desires. Along the way, we'll learn about some of the many spiritual blessings, the wonderful treasures God says He has already given us (Ephesians 1:3). These spiritual treasures are ours for the taking! We'll learn how to embrace them and experience them and apply them to our daily lives. We'll discover how they can help us live strong and fulfill the glorious and abundant life God has called us to. A life lived for Him.

You might want to start by setting aside some time to read the book of Ephesians straight through. Then use these daily readings to deepen your understanding of key verses and themes.

Scripture reminds us, "You are a chosen people, a royal priesthood, a holy nation, God's special possession, that you may declare the praises of him who called you out of darkness into his wonderful light" (1 Peter 2:9).

We are God's people, chosen for greatness. Every day, we can choose to live in the reality of this truth. We can choose to live up to our high and holy calling. We can choose to live our lives for Jesus Christ—the One who laid down His life for us—and bring glory and honor to His name.

Let's make that choice together as we pray through Ephesians!

YOU'RE A **SAINT!**

❝ *Paul, an apostle of Christ Jesus by the will of God, to God's holy people in Ephesus, the faithful in Christ Jesus: Grace and peace to you from God our Father and the Lord Jesus Christ.* ❞

—Ephesians 1:1–2

As Paul begins his letter to the Ephesians, he greets them as "God's holy people." The New King James Version translates this word as "saints." Most people would say a saint is a person of exceptional holiness, someone particularly pious. Church tradition recognized as saints individuals who displayed supernatural power, worked miracles, or suffered a martyr's death. Specific days were set aside to honor these men and women, including November 1—All Saints' Day—a special holiday instituted by Pope Gregory III between AD 730 and 740. The lives and deaths of more than ten thousand people have been celebrated this way. Today the word *saint* is often used to describe a good person. If you do something very kind or thoughtful or unselfish, someone might say to you, "Oh, you're a saint!"

But none of these definitions accurately and completely reflects the biblical view of sainthood. The Greek word translated "saint" means set apart—as in someone who has been brought into relationship with God and is designated by Him as having a sacred purpose or special significance to Him.

So a saint is a person who has been separated from the world, set apart and consecrated to the worship of God. These saints are often referred to throughout the Old and New Testaments. But they're not people who are extra holy or super-pious. Biblical synonyms for the word translated "saint" include *chosen ones, vessels of God, the righteous, believers, Christians*. That's right, Christians. You and me. "And you also were included in Christ when you heard the message of truth, the gospel of your salvation" (Ephesians 1:13).

When we give our hearts to Christ, we are drawn out and set apart from the world and its sinful ways. We no longer walk in rebellion against or disobedience to God. Instead, we have been consecrated (dedicated or devoted) to the worship of God. "You are a chosen generation, a royal priesthood, a holy nation, His own special people, that you may proclaim the praises of Him who called you out of darkness into His marvelous light" (1 Peter 2:9 NKJV).

Each of us is called to this enormous privilege, this tremendous responsibility. No matter where our life leads us, no matter what skills or talents or education we have, no matter what career or ministry we find ourselves in, our one true calling is to glorify God. To praise and worship Him, with all that is in us—all that we have and all that we are and ever will be.

So Paul says to the church at Ephesus: "I urge you to live a life worthy of the calling you have received" (Ephesians 4:1).

Or as Peter put it, "Don't slip back into your old ways of living to satisfy your own desires. You didn't know any better then. But now you must be holy in everything you do, just as God who chose you is holy" (1 Peter 1:14–15 NLT).

In other words, remember who you are. Remember *whose* you are. You are a saint. So live strong and act like one!

REFLECT

What do you think it means to be "holy" or set apart from the world, in a very real, practical sense? *To move through your day confronting, engaging, loving people with a discerning heart that comes from having a tightly knitted relationship w/ God.*

What does being "holy" look like in your life today?
Thinking before I act. Listening to that still voice before I move forward. Accepting others who think, look, act differently than me. Longing to know & be w/ God more. Being transparent about who I am.

PRAY

Heavenly Father, thank You that You chose me to be Your disciple. You have made me one of Your "saints"—setting me apart as Your very own. I belong to You. Teach me what it means to be separate from the world, to be holy. Help me to be faithful and obedient to You.

I want to live a strong life, worthy of my sacred calling. A life that brings joy to Your heart. A life that brings glory and honor to You. Fill me with Your grace and peace today. In Jesus' precious name, I pray. Amen.

ALL I HAVE **NEEDED**

> 66 *Praise be to the God and Father of our Lord Jesus Christ, who has blessed us in the heavenly realms with every spiritual blessing in Christ.* 99

—Ephesians 1:3

Maybe you've seen the cartoon that features a puzzled young woman talking to the bank manager. She asks, "How can I be out of money? I still have checks!"

Balancing the checkbook, juggling the bills—these days it's not easy to make ends meet. Some of us are pinching pennies until they squeal! We don't know how we're going to make it to the end of the month. And it's not just our finances. We're pressed for time, energy, and solutions to our family problems or crises at work. Wisdom to make good choices. Strength to resist temptation. Peace to calm our fears.

The good news is that even when our resources run low—or run out—we have somewhere to turn. We need only to ask our heavenly Father. In Psalm 50:10, God reminds us that He owns the cattle on a thousand hills. He also owns the hills, as well as every blade of grass on those hills and the sun that warms it! The universe and everything in it belongs to Him. His resources are endless. He owns it all. And out of His great love and kindness, our Father generously provides for us, His children. What's His is ours.

Philippians 4:19 tells us, "God will meet all your needs according to the riches of his glory in Christ Jesus." He provides for our physical needs and our spiritual needs.

Sometimes God provides what we need miraculously— money in an unmarked envelope, groceries on the doorstep, a canceled meeting that opens up precious time in our schedule. The creative inspiration or the problem-solving solution we've been searching for. Wisdom, encouragement, direction, victory. Sometimes He shows us how to make better use of the resources He's already given us. And sometimes He helps us see the difference between what we really want and what we truly need. But no matter what, our Father never abandons us, never forsakes us (Hebrews 13:5). He always answers when we call.

Whenever you feel your resources are stretched to their limits, turn to the One whose supplies are limitless.

He giveth more grace when the burdens grow greater,
He sendeth more strength when the labors increase,
To added affliction He addeth His mercies,
To multiplied trials His multiplied peace.

When we have exhausted our store of endurance,

When our strength has failed ere the day is half done,

When we reach the end of our hoarded resources,

Our Father's full giving is only begun.

His love has no limit, His grace has no measure,

His power no boundary known unto men;

But out of His infinite riches in Jesus

He giveth and giveth and giveth again.

—Annie Johnston Flint

REFLECT

What do you need most today?

TO GET OUT OF DEBT

Are you willing to believe God—to trust Him to meet that need? *YES.*

PRAY

Praise You, Father! You have blessed me in the heavenly realms with every spiritual blessing in Christ. You have given me everything I need for life and godliness. Thank You for the physical blessings too. You provide for my daily needs. All I have needed, Your hands have provided. Great is Your faithfulness, Lord, unto me.

FREELY **GIVEN**

> " *For he chose us in him before the creation of the world to be holy and blameless in his sight. In love he predestined us for adoption to sonship through Jesus Christ, in accordance with his pleasure and will—to the praise of his glorious grace, which he has freely given us in the One he loves.* "

—Ephesians 1:4–6

What keeps you from sharing your faith with your unsaved friends and neighbors? In Matthew 28:19–20, Jesus said, "Therefore go and make disciples of all nations, baptizing them in the name of the Father and of the Son and of the Holy Spirit, and teaching them to obey everything I have commanded you."

This Great Commission is for all believers, not just those with the gift of evangelism. In Acts 1:8, Jesus told His disciples, "You will be my witnesses in Jerusalem, and in all Judea and Samaria, and to the ends of the earth."

Sharing our faith is such an awesome privilege and responsibility! So what keeps us from doing what Jesus said? A lot of people admit they're afraid they might "do it wrong"—they're not sure they know all the right things to say when sharing their faith with others. It's easy to forget that at the most basic level, a "witness" is simply one who tells others what he has seen or heard.

One of the most powerful ways to share the gospel is to follow the instructions Jesus gave to a man He had just healed in Mark 5:19: "Go home to your own people and tell them how much the Lord has done for you."

What has He done for you? Well, for starters, before the foundation of the world, God chose you to be His child. He chose you for greatness. He created you and He set you apart as belonging to Him. He adopted you and welcomed you into His family. He saved you from sin.

To be a witness for the Lord, you don't have to quote the words of noted scholars and theologians. You don't have to have memorized all the verses in any particular evangelistic plan. The main thing is to share simply, openly, and honestly what you have experienced for yourself—introducing others to the Savior you have come to know and love. Where would you be without Him? Where will others be?

Jesus said, "Freely you have received; freely give" (Matthew 10:8).

REFLECT

What is your testimony—your witness—your story? How
would you share it in a sentence or two? *I can't remember a
life w/out Jesus because I known & loved him for so
long, but everyday I see him show up in some way new & I
fall in love with him even more.*
What's the longer version of your testimony?

PRAY

*Father, I can't even begin to understand why You chose me to be Your
child before the creation of the world. You created me to be holy—
set apart as belonging to You and blameless in Your sight.*

*I thank You that in Your love, You predestined me to be adopted into
Your family through Your Son, Jesus Christ, according to Your pleasure
and will—the praise of Your glorious grace, which You have so freely
given me in the One You love. Help me to boldly, courageously,
lovingly, and freely share the good news of the gospel
with those You send me today.*

SORRY ISN'T **ENOUGH**

> " *In him we have redemption through his blood, the forgiveness of sins, in accordance with the riches of God's grace that he lavished on us.* "

—Ephesians 1:7–8

Oswald Chambers once said, "We trample the blood of the Son of God underfoot if we think we are forgiven because we are sorry for our sins. The only reason for the forgiveness of our sins by God, and the infinite depth of His promise to forget them, is the death of Jesus Christ."[1]

And what a brutal, agonizing death it was. First He was mocked and ridiculed. Spat upon. Beaten with fists and with whips. His back ripped to ribbons. His brow bruised and bloody from the crown of thorns pressed into His flesh. Nailed to a cross, a sword piercing His side.

Why did Jesus submit to such awful suffering? Why did He allow Himself to undergo such torture, misery, and death? In a word, sin. Not His. Ours! Jesus Himself was without sin. He was perfect, spotless, sinless.

But we are not. Every one of us is a sinner. Each of us has ignored the commandments of our Creator, rejected His authority over us, disobeyed His law, and failed to live up to His holy standards.

Sin has a hefty price tag—death. The death of our bodies, but more importantly, the death of our spirits. We were given immortal souls, designed to live forever. We were meant to experience a deep and meaningful relationship with the One who created us. But nothing sinful or imperfect can ever enter the presence of God. So when we choose sin rather than God, we are choosing eternal separation from Him.

Being sorry isn't enough to fix that.

In His infinite mercy, our Creator made a way for us to be reconciled to Him. God sent His only Son, Jesus, to die in our place—to take the punishment for us, to pay the penalty for our sin.

Why would Jesus do such a thing?

Love. Love for you. Love for me. Love for the whole human race. "For God so loved the world that he gave his one and only Son, that whoever believes in him shall not perish but have eternal life" (John 3:16).

The crucifixion was no surprise to Jesus. He knew it was coming all along. From the beginning He understood what He would suffer. Yet He deliberately chose the path that would lead to the cross. He willingly laid down His life to save us.

The blood of Jesus was shed for us. That day on the cross,

He paid the ultimate price in order to reconcile God and man—to make peace between the two. What appeared to be a tragedy borne of hate was in fact love's greatest triumph. And the crucifixion was not the end of the story. Death had no legal claim on Jesus—He had done nothing to deserve to die. So death could not keep Him in the grave. On the morning of the third day, He rose again in power and glory. And now He lives forevermore!

Because Jesus lives, so can we. Because of the suffering that Jesus endured, because of His death on the cross, because of His resurrection, the power of sin has been broken. Death has been conquered. We have forgiveness, redemption, the hope of heaven, the gift of eternal life. The riches of God's grace lavished on us.

How can we ever thank Him enough?

REFLECT

When was the last time you thanked God—truly, earnestly, sincerely thanked Him—for the forgiveness that cost Jesus His life?

PRAY

Lord Jesus, once again I confess that I am a sinner in need of a Savior. I know it was my sin that sent You to the cross. You took the punishment in my place. Thank You for sacrificing Your life for mine. Thank You for saving me from death and giving me eternal life. In You I have redemption through Your blood, the forgiveness of sins, the riches of God's grace that He lavished on me. Help me live my life in a way that brings glory and honor to You. Amen.

ALL PART OF THE **PLAN**

> ❝ *In him we were also chosen, having been predestined according to the plan of him who works out everything in conformity with the purpose of his will, in order that we, who were the first to put our hope in Christ, might be for the praise of his glory.* ❞

—Ephesians 1:11-12

It's a theme often repeated in Scripture: God has a purpose, a plan. He is working everything out according to His will. Probably the most familiar passage on the subject is Romans 8:28–29: "And we know that in all things God works for the good of those who love him, who have been called according to his purpose. For those God foreknew he also predestined to be conformed to the image of his Son."

This passage has both comforted and challenged believers for centuries. What exactly does it mean that in *all things* God works for the *good*? Looking back, we've experienced some pretty unhappy things. Heartbreaking things. Even evil things.

There are shameful things we've done and shameful things that have been done to us. How could it be that things that make no earthly sense somehow have heavenly purpose and meaning?

The answer lies in the sovereignty of God. The word *sovereignty* means having supreme, unlimited power or authority, complete control. To be sovereign is to be preeminent; indisputable; greatest in degree; utmost or extreme; above all others in character, importance, and excellence.

Colossians 1:15–18 says of Jesus:

> The Son is the image of the invisible God, the firstborn over all creation. For in him all things were created: things in heaven and on earth. . . . He is before all things, and in him all things hold together. And he is the head of the body, the church; he is the beginning and the firstborn . . . so that in everything he might have the supremacy.

Because Jesus is all of these things, although evil is prevalent and we live in a fallen world, He has the power and the authority and the ability to cause all things to work together for our good—just as it says in Romans 8:28. Remember that when God talks about "the good of those who love him," He doesn't mean our immediate comfort or happiness. He means that He is making us more and more like Jesus, which will ultimately give us the greatest joy now and in eternity.

Author, preacher, and Bible teacher John Piper points out that God was able to take the most "spectacular" sin (the greatest evil, the most wicked injustice) in the history of the world—the crucifixion of Jesus—and use it to triumph over the devil, redeem His children, and glorify His Son.[2]

> When you were dead in your sins . . . God made you alive with Christ. He forgave us all our sins, having canceled the charge of our legal indebtedness, which stood against us and condemned us; he has taken it away, nailing it to the cross. And having disarmed the powers and authorities, he made a public spectacle of them, triumphing over them by the cross. (Colossians 2:13–15)

The metaphor here suggests a victorious Roman general leading his captives—the physical evidence of his complete and total victory—through the streets for all the people to see.

God has a plan, a purpose, a will that He is actively working to accomplish in the world today. In your life today. And it will be done! Because nothing is too difficult for Him.

REFLECT

What things do you need to trust God to work together for good in your life so that you can live strong today?

My memory and ability to focus my thoughts to achieve the plans He has for me. The next adventure He has planned for me.

PRAY

Lord, I thank You that You chose me before time began to be a part of Your plan. I trust You with everything that concerns me today. I know that You will work out everything for my good and Your glory. You work through the ages, through time and space to accomplish the plan You had from the beginning. You cause all things to conform to the purpose of Your will. May all of us who were the first to hope in Christ continually bring You praise, glory, and honor.

THE TRUTH
AND **NOTHING BUT**

❝ *And you also were included in Christ when you heard the message of truth, the gospel of your salvation. When you believed, you were marked in him with a seal, the promised Holy Spirit, who is a deposit guaranteeing our inheritance until the redemption of those who are God's possession—to the praise of his glory.* **❞**

—Ephesians 1:13–14

Have you heard it said, "The truth will set you free"? A lot of people seem to be quoting that scripture these days, often right before revealing some incredibly hurtful secret, a nasty criticism, or a sweeping judgment. And in the aftermath that wreaks havoc in the lives of everyone around them, you have to wonder: How could that scripture be true?

Well, let's go back and look at that verse in context. In John 8:31–32, Jesus said: "If you hold to my teaching, you are really my disciples. Then you will know the truth, and the truth will set you free."

If you hold to my teaching . . .

If you study the Scriptures, if you meditate on God's Word, if you take them to heart, you will begin to know and recognize and understand God's truth. And God's truth is what will set you free.

It may be very true that your parents never wanted you. That truth won't set you free. But God's truth says He wanted you. He chose you. He loves you (Psalm 139; Ephesians 1:3–5). Now *that* truth will set you free.

It may be true that many of the people you love and trust will disappoint you or hurt you, abandon you or betray you. Again, it may be true, but not helpful. Here's a truth that *is* helpful: God says He will never abandon you or forsake you (Hebrews 13:5). Even if you are unfaithful to Him, He will be faithful to you (2 Timothy 2:13).

It may be true that you are a terrible sinner, a rotten, miserable person. That truth by itself won't set you free. But this one will: "If we confess our sins, he is faithful and just and will forgive us our sins and purify us from all unrighteousness" (1 John 1:9). "If anyone is in Christ, the new creation has come: The old has gone, the new is here!" (2 Corinthians 5:17). Satan has no claim on you. Jesus purchased you with His own blood. And there's evidence: you have been marked with the seal of the Holy Spirit—proof of your authenticity as a child of God, proof of His ownership of you, of your belonging to Him.

So hold fast to Jesus' teachings. Hold fast to the truth. Let God's truth—the whole truth and nothing but the truth—set you free today!

REFLECT

What aspect of God's truth do you most need to grab hold of today? *THAT HE IS SUFFICIENT. I TEND TO WANT TO GRAB HOLD OF THE REIGNS & STEER INSTEAD OF JUST RIDING THE HORSE W/ABANDON.*

PRAY

Lord, help me hold fast to Your truth and not fall for the lies of the enemy. I have heard the word of truth, the gospel of my salvation, and I have believed it. I have believed You. Thank You for marking me with a seal, the promised Holy Spirit who testifies that I am Yours. Your Spirit living and working in me is a deposit guaranteeing my inheritance until the day when You redeem all those who are Your possession.
I look forward to that day—I long for that day. I praise You and glorify Your name.

THANK **GOD!**

“ *For this reason, ever since I heard about your faith in the Lord Jesus and your love for all God's people, I have not stopped giving thanks for you, remembering you in my prayers. I keep asking that the God of our Lord Jesus Christ, the glorious Father, may give you the Spirit of wisdom and revelation, so that you may know him better.* ”

—Ephesians 1:15–17

Think of the people who have made a positive difference in your life, especially those who have affected your spiritual life. What was it about them? Was it something they said or did? The time they spent? The example they set? The prayers they offered on your behalf?

Imagine where you would be without them. And thank God for sending them to you, for putting them in your path! Pray that He will be with them and bless them today.

Now think about the people you encounter on a daily basis, the lives you touch: your family, your friends, neighbors, coworkers, members of your church and community. Are you consciously reaching out to them and making a difference in their lives?

The apostle John realized what a great honor, what an amazing privilege it was to lead others to Jesus and to disciple (teach and train) them in their faith. He said, "I have no greater joy than to hear that my children are walking in the truth" (3 John 4).

The apostle Paul could relate. He said to the believers in Colossae:

> We always thank God, the Father of our Lord Jesus Christ, when we pray for you, because we have heard of your faith in Christ Jesus and of the love you have for all God's people—the faith and love that spring from the hope stored up for you in heaven and about which you have already heard in the true message of the gospel that has come to you. In the same way, the gospel is bearing fruit and growing throughout the whole world. (Colossians 1:3–6)

It's amazing to see God working in the hearts of those around us, to watch them grow deeper in their relationship with Him and learn to live strong in Him—especially when we have a part in it! We can't help but be filled with joy and thanksgiving.

Want to experience this joy more often? Keep your eyes open! Look for people you can lead to Jesus. Look for brothers and sisters in Christ you can encourage in their faith. It could be something you say or something you do. It might be the time and resources you invest, or the example you set. It may be your fervent and faithful prayers on their behalf. Give it some thought: "Therefore, as we have opportunity, let us do good to all people, especially to those who belong to the family of believers" (Galatians 6:10). Thank God for these people. And pray that they continue to grow closer to Jesus, day by day.

REFLECT

Express your appreciation for what others have done for you by paying it forward. Who can you bless or encourage or reach out to today? *Doe, Ashlee, Ann*

PRAY

Dear Jesus, thank You for calling me to a love relationship with You. Thank You for making me a part of Your family, the family of God. Thank You for each person who has pointed me to You, each person who has taught me, challenged me, encouraged me, inspired me, and helped me to grow in my faith.

Lord, thank You for each life You have given me the privilege of pointing to You, each person I am able to teach or challenge or encourage or inspire. There is no greater joy than to see them grow in their faith and in Your love.

Be with all of my brothers and sisters in Christ. Give them the Spirit of wisdom and revelation, so that they may know You better and live strong in You. Bless them today, I pray.

REVELATION AND **TRANSFORMATION**

> ❝ *I pray that the eyes of your heart may be enlightened in order that you may know the hope to which he has called you, the riches of his glorious inheritance in his holy people, and his incomparably great power for us who believe.* ❞

—Ephesians 1:18–19

Have you made choices in your past that you deeply regret? Are there things you still struggle with today? Perhaps in your heart of hearts, you long to do great things for God, but you wonder, How could He possibly use someone like me?

If you do, guess what? You're in good company. The Bible is chock-full of messed-up, mixed-up people—whom God still used! Think about it: Abraham was a coward. Jacob was a liar. Moses was a hothead. Rahab was a prostitute. David was an adulterer. Jonah was a whiner. Matthew was a cheater. Martha was a busybody. Thomas was a doubter. Prior to his conversion, the apostle Paul was a Pharisee who killed Christians in the name of God.

These men and women were all too human. They had serious character flaws. They made major mistakes. But God chose them for greatness and worked in them and through them to accomplish great and mighty things for His kingdom. In 2 Corinthians 4:7, Paul explains, "We have this treasure in jars of clay to show that this all-surpassing power is from God and not from us." Through the cracks in our broken, messed-up lives, God's light shines brightly. The world can see Jesus at work in us. This is the hope to which He has called us, the hope to which He wants to call others through us—the gift of salvation and eternal life.

Even so, some of us struggle to get past our past. We may find ourselves still battling things we thought we'd overcome or should have overcome long ago. There is still hope: In 2 Corinthians 12:7, the apostle Paul talks about wrestling with a "thorn in [his] flesh." Beginning in verse 8, he says: "Three times I pleaded with the Lord to take it away from me. But he said to me, 'My grace is sufficient for you, for my power is made perfect in weakness.'" Paul goes on to say, "Therefore I will boast all the more gladly about my weaknesses, so that Christ's power may rest on me. That is why, for Christ's sake, I delight in weaknesses, in insults, in hardships, in persecutions, in difficulties. For when I am weak, then I am strong."

See, we don't have to be perfect or pious or put-together. We just need to be willing and available, so we can say, like Isaiah, "Here am I. Send me!" (Isaiah 6:8).

Each and every day, God uses ordinary people like us to do extraordinary things for Him.

REFLECT

What keeps you from saying to God today, "Here am I. Send me!"? *Financial concerns, insecurity & my ability to communicate well.*

Do you believe in His power to transform your heart and mind, to change your life, to use your story for His glory? *I rest in it & constantly look for ways to further my relationship w/ God so I walk confidently in his power.*

PRAY

Thank You for saving me, redeeming me, and transforming me.
I can't even begin to grasp all You are doing in me and through me.
Truly Your power is made perfect in my weakness.

Lord, open the eyes of my heart. Give me a revelation of the hope to which You have called me and help me never to lose sight of it. Teach me to appropriate the riches of Your glorious inheritance—the spiritual trust, the family legacy that is mine. I want to experience Your incomparably great power in my life today so that I can live strong for You.
Lord, I believe.

ABOVE **ALL**

> ❝ *That power is the same as the mighty strength he exerted when he raised Christ from the dead and seated him at his right hand in the heavenly realms, far above all rule and authority, power and dominion, and every name that is invoked, not only in the present age but also in the one to come.* ❞

—Ephesians 1:19–21

A centurion came to Jesus to ask Him to heal a beloved servant who was sick and at the point of death. But when Jesus prepared to go to the Roman soldier's home, the man replied,

> Lord, I do not deserve to have you come under my roof. But just say the word, and my servant will be healed. For I myself am a man under authority, with soldiers under me. I tell this one, "Go," and he goes; and that one, "Come," and he comes. (Matthew 8:8–9)

The centurion recognized that Jesus had authority—authority that had been given to Him by God the Father. Whatever Jesus commanded would be done, whether He was there personally or not. It wasn't what Jesus physically did or said that brought healing. It was the authority He had. Jesus said, "All authority in heaven and on earth has been given to me" (Matthew 28:18).

Philippians 2:9–11 explains,

> God exalted him to the highest place and gave him the name that is above every name, that at the name of Jesus every knee should bow, in heaven and on earth and under the earth, and every tongue acknowledge that Jesus Christ is Lord, to the glory of God the Father.

The natural world submitted to Jesus' authority: the wind and the waves obeyed Him. The fig tree withered and died at His command. In the physical realm, Jesus exercised authority over sickness and disease. He healed the blind, the lame, and the deaf. The spirit world acknowledged Him—demons trembled in His presence and begged Him not to torture them.

Jesus had the power to read people's thoughts and reveal their hearts. He had the authority to forgive sin. Jesus had control of His own destiny. He said, "No one takes [my life] from me, but I lay it down of my own accord" (John 10:18). He had authority over death and hell—it couldn't keep Him in the

grave. Now He's seated at the right hand of the Father, the King
of kings and Lord of lords. And He calls *us* His friends.

REFLECT

Is Jesus "Lord" of every part of your heart and life today? In
every relationship, situation, and circumstance? *make Him Lord daily in my life* *I wish I
could say "yes" completely but I try to grab
things back from Him all the time. It is my
hearts desire to.*
Are there some people or things you still need to surrender

to Him—attitudes, behaviors, or choices you need to bring

under His rule? *My fear of being alone in this
world. Fear of not measuring up mentally to be
able to be successful in the things I attempt
to accomplish.*

PRAY

God, I'm in awe of Your incomparably great power, the mighty strength
that You exerted in Christ when You raised Him from the dead and seated
Him at Your right hand in the heavenly realms. You have made Him far
above all rule and authority, power and dominion, and every title that
can be given, now and forever. He is the King of kings and the Lord of

lords. One day every knee will bow before Him, and every tongue will acknowledge His name. I'm so grateful for the privilege of knowing Him, loving Him, serving Him, and worshiping Him now. I surrender my heart to You, to Him, freely, joyfully, and enthusiastically today!

DEAD MAN **WALKING**

" *As for you, you were dead in your transgressions and sins, in which you used to live when you followed the ways of this world and of the ruler of the kingdom of the air, the spirit who is now at work in those who are disobedient. All of us also lived among them at one time, gratifying the cravings of our flesh and following its desires and thoughts. Like the rest, we were by nature deserving of wrath.* **"**

—Ephesians 2:1-3

"D ead man walking! Dead man walking!"

Years ago, prison guards used to warn each other and any nearby inmates that the prisoner they were escorting down the hallway had been condemned to die. In the eyes of the law, this prisoner was already dead. He had run out of chances, exhausted any appeals. The court had determined he was beyond rehabilitation, beyond redemption—completely and utterly doomed. Such a man had nothing left to lose and must be considered extremely dangerous, especially desperate.

Scripture tells us that we are all born "dead men walking." The sinful nature we inherited from our first parents, Adam and Eve, tainted the entire human race. And daily we prove that if we had been in the garden of Eden, we would have made the same choice—we would have fallen too. Our own thoughts, our own attitudes, our actions and behaviors testify against us.

In Ephesians 4:18–19, Paul describes the futility of our thinking:

> Their minds are full of darkness; they wander far from the life God gives because they have closed their minds and hardened their hearts against him. They have no sense of shame. They live for lustful pleasure and eagerly practice every kind of impurity. (NLT)

Our sin separates us from God, keeps us apart from Him, and cuts us off from a relationship with Him. We call that separation "death"—spiritual death, and eventually physical death and eternal death.

Yet blindly we follow the ways of the world. We succumb to the seduction of the "ruler of the kingdom of the air" (Ephesians 2:2)—the ruler of the demons in the spirit world. As if our own pride, our own selfishness, and our own greed and lust weren't enough to contend with, we have an enemy constantly tempting us and luring us to our death.

Sounds pretty hopeless, doesn't it?

Like a prisoner on death row.

But thanks to Jesus, we are not without hope. We are not beyond forgiveness—we are not beyond redemption. "There is now no condemnation for those who are in Christ Jesus" (Romans 8:1). We have been declared "not guilty"—when we know we are! How is this possible?

"He was pierced for our transgressions, he was crushed for our iniquities; the punishment that brought us peace was on him, and by his wounds we are healed" (Isaiah 53:5).

The death sentence has been lifted, because the penalty has already been paid by Someone else. Jesus died so we could live.

REFLECT

What kind of emotion, what kind of attitude or outlook would you expect to find in a death-row inmate who had been pardoned and set free to live a new life? *Gratitude that knows no end. A need to give back to the one who has redeemed you.*

Is that same emotion or attitude or outlook reflected in your own life today? *I wake each day thankful for all that has been done of give to me. I realize I owe my all because of what Jesus has done for me.*

PRAY

*Lord Jesus, I shudder to think that I was once dead in my transgressions
and sins—I used to walk in rebellion and disobedience. I lived only to
please myself. In my ignorance, I was ruled by the power of the enemy
and didn't even know it. I was under a death sentence.
I deserved Your judgment and wrath.*

*But in Your love, You rescued me from darkness. You set me free from
bondage to sin. You brought me out of the enemy's camp and made me
one of Your own. You raised me to life—eternal life. With all that
is in me, I praise You and worship You. I bless Your holy name.*

HE **LIVES!**

> 66 *But because of his great love for us, God, who is rich in mercy, made us alive with Christ even when we were dead in transgressions—it is by grace you have been saved. And God raised us up with Christ and seated us with him in the heavenly realms in Christ Jesus, in order that in the coming ages he might show the incomparable riches of his grace, expressed in his kindness to us in Christ Jesus.* 99

—Ephesians 2:4-7

A few years ago, I had the privilege of touring the Holy Land with a group of Christian journalists. It was an incredible experience . . . so many familiar scriptures took on deeper meaning as we were able to put them into cultural, historical, and geographical context. But by far, the most meaningful experience for me was our brief visit to the Garden Tomb.

So many of the traditional "religious" sites we visited were dark and dismal places—shrouded by centuries of religious superstition and empty ritual worship. In order to accept that the place was what it claimed to be, one would have to completely disregard the biblical account of what supposedly took place there—or twist the Scriptures to make it fit, accepting the traditions of men over the truth of the Word.

But in the peaceful beauty of the Garden Tomb, it was a different story. The chaplain led us from place to place around the garden, sharing scriptures with us and pointing out how in every respect, what we were looking at matched the biblical account perfectly. "This is what the Bible says . . . and this is what we find." It was so simple and beautiful and faith-affirming. Our tour ended at the tomb itself. After explaining traditional burial customs and reminding us of the description of this place in the Gospels, our guide concluded, "But you know, you've come all this way to see nothing. The tomb is empty. 'He is not here; he has risen, just as he said'" (Matthew 28:6).

Hallelujah! Our hope is not in pilgrimages to sacred sites, ancient altars, and man-made monuments. Our faith is built on the reality of Jesus' resurrection. Our trust is in our risen Savior, Jesus Christ our Lord.

The same God who raised Him from the dead has raised us up from death (spiritual and physical) to life (eternal). "I have been crucified with Christ and I no longer live, but Christ lives in me. The life I now live in the body, I live by faith in the Son of God, who loved me and gave himself for me" (Galatians 2:20).

Our past is over and done with; our glorious future awaits!

REFLECT

How are you living by faith today? *Believing that God knows what's ahead for me in my day & has prepared me to step in to whatever he has ahead.*

In what circumstances are you dependent on the mercy and grace of God—on His kindness to you through Jesus, His Son? *That He still chases after me when I continue to hold onto controlling, prideful ways.*

PRAY

Father, because of Your great love, in Your rich and abundant mercy, You have made us alive with Christ—even when we were dead in our sins. By Your grace You saved us and raised us up with Christ and seated us with Him in the heavenly realms. You gave us new life here and now, and heaven for all eternity—revealing the incomparable riches of Your grace, expressed in Your kindness to us in Christ Jesus.

My hope is in You. My faith is in You. My life is in You. I worship You and bless Your holy name.

NOTHING BUT THE **BLOOD**

66 *For it is by grace you have been saved, through faith—and this is not from yourselves, it is the gift of God.* 99

—Ephesians 2:8

These days it seems we're constantly inundated with advertisements for cleaning products. With the incredible power of oxygen or citrus fruit or chemical agents, they claim to remove "even the toughest stains" from any surface under any circumstance, no matter how old, how dark, how deep, or how dismal. Some of these products are rather remarkable. It's too bad none of these amazing liquids or powders can make us feel clean inside, erase the wounds to our spirits, wipe away the mistakes of our past, or wash out the stain of our sin.

Like Shakespeare's Lady Macbeth, we are desperate to rid ourselves of the tell-tale sign of our guilt. We go to elaborate lengths to camouflage and cover up and hide our shame. We try everything we can think of—all the activities, behaviors, and products that promise to purify. Yet despite our best, most concentrated efforts, the stain of sin remains.

And we're not alone. The truth is, "There is no one righteous, not even one" (Romans 3:10).

When we finally reach the end of our own futile efforts, we fall on our faces before God, knowing we deserve His wrath and judgment. And then we hear Him say, "Come now, let us settle the matter. . . . Though your sins are like scarlet, they shall be as white as snow" (Isaiah 1:18).

God applies His very own "super stain remover" to our hearts—the blood of Jesus, His Son. "If we confess our sins, he is faithful and just and will forgive us our sins and purify us from all unrighteousness" (1 John 1:9). The blood of Jesus gets out the most stubborn spots; it removes the darkest stains. It completely removes our guilt and shame and makes us pure again.

In the words of the old hymn by Robert Lowry:

What can wash away my sin?
Nothing but the blood of Jesus;
What can make me whole again?
Nothing but the blood of Jesus.

Nothing can for sin atone,
Nothing but the blood of Jesus;
Naught of good that I have done,
Nothing but the blood of Jesus.

Oh! precious is the flow

That makes me white as snow;

No other fount I know,

Nothing but the blood of Jesus.

Our salvation cost Jesus everything, but to us it's free—all we have to do is receive it by faith and believe in His name.

REFLECT

In what specific ways can you receive God's grace—embrace it, experience it, apply it—in your own life today?

There are days I move forward doing things w/out about God, asking for his wisdom, power & presence. I'm running things out of my own skill set & control. I need His patience with this side of me & His help in turning these things over daily

PRAY

Lord Jesus, thank You for dying on the cross to save me from my sin. I know I didn't do anything to deserve such amazing love, such a costly and precious sacrifice. There's no way I could ever earn my salvation. I'm not good enough. No one is. It's only by Your mercy, Your grace, that I've been saved through faith. And even my faith isn't my own achievement or accomplishment or virtue—it's a gift from You! You have chosen me for greatness and given me Your beauty, Your purity, Your perfection—Your righteousness, right-standing with God. Thank You, with all my heart.

HEART**WARMING**

❝ . . . not by works, so that no one can boast. ❞

—Ephesians 2:9

For the first thirty years of his life, Charles Wesley thought he knew all about being a devoted Christian. The Wesleys counted many prominent preachers, Bible teachers, and theologians in their family. Their children learned Greek, Hebrew, and Latin, just as their parents had, so that they could read the Bible in its original languages.

Charles and his brother John went to Oxford University, where they started "The Holy Club." They hoped to set an example for the other students, encouraging them to live a disciplined Christian life. Club members committed themselves to getting up early for personal prayer and Bible study, meeting regularly for worship services, and ministering to the poor and downtrodden. The Holy Club members were so sincere and earnest, so systematic and methodical in the practice of their faith, that others started referring to them as "methodists."

But as hard as the brothers tried to be devout and godly, they never felt they were good enough. In their zeal, they were always trying harder, looking for new ways to prove their devotion, to somehow earn God's favor and show themselves worthy of His love.

In 1735, the Wesleys accepted an invitation to travel to Georgia. John would serve as a military chaplain and Charles would be secretary to the governor. Both brothers saw themselves as missionaries. They particularly hoped to reach the native people as well as the settlers living in the area. But the trip was a disaster. The brothers returned home disillusioned and discouraged.

Charles realized he had no peace and no joy in his Christian life. He felt no assurance of his salvation. He was often afraid to fall asleep at night, fearing he might die. What if his best efforts had not been good enough to meet with God's approval? What if it was hell that awaited him, and not heaven?

While recovering from a lengthy illness, Charles began to read the writings of Martin Luther on the scriptures that teach "the righteous will live by faith" (Galatians 3:11) and we're saved through our faith in Jesus, not our good works (Ephesians 2:8–9). At the same time, Charles met some Christians who spoke of the assurance of salvation that comes from having a personal encounter and relationship with Jesus.

Charles called this experience his "heartwarming." His heart was not only warmed by the love of Jesus, but it was filled to overflowing with awe and gratitude and praise. Almost immediately, he began writing hymns to express his heartfelt worship, such as this one:

> And can it be that I should gain
> an int'rest in the Savior's blood?
> Died He for me, who caused His pain?
> For me, who Him to death pursued?
> Amazing love! How can it be
> that Thou, my God, shouldst die for me?

A few days after Charles opened his heart to Jesus, John did the same. They began preaching with new passion, new conviction, and new authority. In their services, they sang Charles's hymns, which so powerfully captured the life-changing truths of the gospel and so beautifully expressed the believer's response of faith. Hundreds of thousands of people came to trust in Christ as a great revival spread throughout England—not because of anyone's hard work, good deeds, holy living, or sacrificial giving, but because of their faith in God's redeeming grace.

REFLECT

"Nothing you can do will make God love you any more or any less than He does at this very moment." How does your heart respond to this statement? *It's freeing & opens me up to live more transparently & seek Jesus above all else.*

PRAY

Lord Jesus, You have saved me by Your grace—dying on the cross in my place. It is my faith in You—believing in You, trusting in You—that brings me into a personal love relationship with You. It's not by good deeds I do or bad deeds I refrain from doing, or sacrifices that I make for You. I can't boast in any righteousness of my own. My righteousness comes from You alone. Thank You, Jesus.

A **MASTERPIECE**

> 66 *For we are God's handiwork, <u>created in</u>*
> <u>*Christ Jesus to do good works, which God prepared*</u>
> <u>*in advance for us to do.*</u> 99

—Ephesians 2:10

When Amy was a little girl, she didn't like the color of her eyes. To her, they were a plain old brown, while her sister's were a beautiful blue. Amy learned in church that God can do anything—that if we really believe in our hearts and ask Him to do something, He will. So one night at bedtime, she prayed as hard as she knew how that God would turn her brown eyes blue. Then next morning, she ran to the bathroom to look in the mirror, confident that her request had been heard and answered.

Well, it had—but not the way she wanted. God said no. He didn't change the color of Amy's eyes. He left them the color He had made them. And for a time, Amy was heartbroken. She didn't understand. She *couldn't* understand . . . at least, not then.

But many years later, God sent Amy Carmichael as a missionary to India. Dressed in traditional Indian clothing, with her skin stained dark with tea leaves, and her eyes brown, she didn't stand out like a typical European tourist. She looked like a native, blending in with the other women of the community. This made it possible for Amy to slip in and out of Hindu temples unnoticed—and rescue hundreds of little girls who had been sold into slavery and prostitution.

It turned out Amy's brown eyes weren't a random act of genetics—they weren't a punishment or sign that she was any less loved or favored. They were a precious gift from God to help her accomplish His unique plan and purpose for her life. No wonder He wouldn't change them!

"'For I know the plans I have for you,' declares the LORD, 'plans to prosper you and not to harm you, plans to give you hope and a future'" (Jeremiah 29:11).

God says we are His handiwork, His creation, His masterpiece! Over and over, the Scriptures tell us that God made each of us the way we are for a reason. Before we were even born, He had a plan and a purpose for our lives—a specific calling, a certain path He had chosen for us. He has kingdom work for us to do! He has chosen us for greatness and to live strong for Him.

You created my inmost being; you knit me together in my mother's womb. I praise you because I am fearfully and wonderfully made; your works are wonderful, I know that full well. . . . All the days ordained for me were written in your book before one of them came to be. (Psalm 139:13–16)

We may not always appreciate this; often we have our own ideas of how we should look or what we should be like. We think we'd be happier if we had someone else's appearance or personality or gifts. But God knows us best. After all, He created us. And lest we forget, *He* is the potter; we are the clay (Isaiah 64:8; Jeremiah 18:1–6). God molds us and shapes us as He sees fit. We are vessels to be used for His glory. The amazing thing is that He is able to work even with our missteps and mistakes, and turn our weakness into strength. We are precious in His sight. As Amy's story reminds us, we can trust Him, even when we don't understand.

REFLECT

What evidence of God's craftsmanship marks your life—and makes you uniquely you? *Being single @ 54.*

PRAY

Lord, before I was born, You knew me. You knit me together in my mother's womb. Even then, You had a plan and a purpose for me, a calling. I am Your workmanship, Your masterpiece, created to do the work of Your kingdom, work You prepared in advance for me to do. You have called me and equipped me and trained me—You are still calling, equipping, training me—for these very special tasks. Help me to give all that I have and all that I am. Empower me. Enable me to accomplish all You have given me to do and to do it well, for Your glory. Amen.

THE DAY OF **ATONEMENT**

But now in Christ Jesus you who once were far away have been brought near by the blood of Christ. ❞

—Ephesians 2:13

If you look on your calendar for fall, usually in late September or early October, you'll see a note informing you of a Jewish holiday—Yom Kippur. In the Old Testament this holiday was referred to as the Day of Atonement. This was a solemn day of fasting, prayer, and repentance. The nation of Israel gathered together to confess their sins—both corporate and individual—to seek atonement and reconciliation with God.

This was the one and only day of the year that the high priest could step beyond the veil in the temple and enter into the Holy of Holies—the sacred place where the presence of God rested. The priest represented the people and served as a mediator on their behalf. He sacrificed a spotless (perfect) goat or lamb as a sin offering and sprinkled its blood on the Mercy Seat. "In fact, the law requires that nearly everything be

like the empty Seat in the tomb.

cleansed with blood, and without the shedding of blood there is no forgiveness" (Hebrews 9:22).

Outside, the priest laid his hands on another goat and confessed Israel's sin once again. This "scapegoat" was taken outside of town and allowed to wander away in the wilderness, symbolically carrying the people's sins away with him.

Reflecting on these traditional ceremonies, Hebrews 9:13–14 exclaims,

> The blood of goats and bulls and the ashes of a heifer sprinkled on those who are ceremonially unclean sanctify them so that they are outwardly clean. How much more, then, will the blood of Christ, who through the eternal Spirit offered himself unblemished to God, cleanse our consciences from acts that lead to death, so that we may serve the living God!

When Jesus died on the cross, He became a sacrifice for us. He paid the penalty for our sins completely, once and for all. He removed the barrier that separated us from God. He is no longer hidden from us by a heavy veil.

Matthew 27:51 tells us that at the moment Jesus died, "the curtain of the temple was torn in two from top to bottom." Because of the blood of Jesus, we have been given access to the Holy of Holies. We can enter the presence of God without fear or shame. Our sins have been forgiven, blotted out, washed

away in the blood of the Lamb. And thanks to Calvary, a day of
sorrow has become a day of celebration!

REFLECT

Are you living strong in the light of Calvary, experiencing
Christ's forgiveness and the joy that it brings? Or are you trying somehow to atone for your own sins—punishing yourself,
separating yourself, and withdrawing from the God who loves
you and gave Himself for you? *I think I constantly
want to put up my to reflect on what I haven't done
or accomplished & allow it to determine my value rather
leaning into, what God says he thinks of me & wants from
Based on today's scriptures, what do you think God would* me.
say to you?
*↳ He
doesn't want me
to live under the
burden of expectation
but to live w/ expectancy
of what He has in store
& what he is doing now.*

PRAY

*Jesus, I was once so far away from You—lost in darkness, in my sin,
and in sadness. But through Your sacrifice at Calvary, You brought me*

near to the heart of God. You reconciled me to Yourself. You welcomed
me into Your family. You have cleansed me, purified me, forgiven me,
and restored me. I will praise You and worship You all of my days.
I can never thank You enough for Your wonderful, saving love.

HE IS OUR **PEACE**

> ❝ *For he himself is our peace, who has made the two groups one and has destroyed the barrier, the dividing wall of hostility, by setting aside in his flesh the law with its commands and regulations. His purpose was to create in himself one new humanity out of the two, thus making peace, and in one body to reconcile both of them to God through the cross, by which he put to death their hostility.* ❞

—Ephesians 2:14–16

Abraham was a man of exceptional faith, courage, and conviction. God chose him to start a family that would become a tribe, a people, and eventually a nation set apart for God Himself. Out of all the people in the world, they would be God's people. He would teach them to know Him and to walk in His ways. He would nurture them and protect them and provide for them. He would bless those who blessed them and curse those who cursed them. God would hold them up as a shining example of what He wanted all humankind to be—an example of the kind of relationship He longed to have with all the peoples of the earth.

These people came to be known as Hebrews or Israelites or the Jews. From then on, there were two kinds of people: Jews and non-Jews (or Gentiles). People who knew God and followed His law (Jews)—and people who did not (Gentiles). The two groups did not associate with one another, in part because God had called His people to separate themselves and come out from the world, so that they would not be corrupted or compromised. Non-Jews had different beliefs, different values, different customs and cultures. Over time the separation turned to discrimination and prejudice that was practiced and experienced by both groups. Racism. Animosity. Hostility. Conflict.

Jews considered Gentiles inferior because they were ceremonially "unclean." Gentiles didn't observe the law of Moses or any of the ceremonial rules and regulations the rabbis had added to it through the centuries. The exclusivity is almost hard to imagine in our evangelical culture today. But Gentiles were not invited or welcome to worship the One True God—even if they wanted to. Barriers had been built around the inner courts of the temple to keep them out!

This is why it was so astonishing to Jewish believers to learn that the Messiah had not just come for them. He was not only the Savior of the Jews but the Savior of the Gentiles too.

Jesus made it clear that God's salvation and redemption is for everyone who trusts in Him—both Jew and Gentile. He broke through the barriers. He tore down the walls of separation. All believers are now God's children, part of one family, God's family. His chosen people.

"Through the gospel the Gentiles are heirs together with Israel, members together of one body, and sharers together in the promise in Christ Jesus" (Ephesians 3:6).

Our love for God gives us something in common. Because we love Him, we love each other. Where once there was division, hostility, and conflict, there is now unity, brotherhood, and peace. We have been reconciled to God and one another by the Prince of Peace—Jesus Himself.

REFLECT

Are there any walls—barriers—in your heart against other people that shouldn't be there? *I've placed walls of assumptions as to who I think they are & what they believe in regards to other denominations. I'm finding that I need to learn for myself what they believe.*

PRAY

Thank You, Jesus, that You are our peace. You have made us one.
You have destroyed the barriers, the dividing walls of hostility that have
long separated us from God and from one another. On the cross,
You abolished the law with its commandments and regulations.
Because of You, I am free. Free to worship You. Free to love You.
Free to love others. Free to live strong.

Lord, break down any walls in my heart today—barriers between me
and You, barriers between me and my brothers and sisters in Christ.
Help me to live in Your love and to share that love with everyone I meet.

LORD WE NEED YOU TO HAVE US ALL ONE AGAIN IN 4 THROUGH YM. OUR NATION IS BECOMING MORE 4 MORE DIVIDED 4 WE ARE BEYOND BEING ABLE TO DO IT FOR OURSELVES.

OPEN **ARMS**

> ❝ *For through him we both have access to the Father by one Spirit. Consequently, you are no longer foreigners and strangers, but fellow citizens with God's people and also members of his household.* ❞

—Ephesians 2:18-19

Have you ever seen a small child running full speed, almost hurling himself into his father's open arms? No caution, no hesitation, no fear of rejection. Absolute trust. Absolute certainty in belonging, in having the right and the privilege. The child is confident of being welcomed, received, and embraced.

Thanks to Jesus, no matter what your relationship with your earthly father, you can have this kind of trusting, loving relationship with your heavenly Father. Once we were outsiders, outcasts, alienated from God by our rebellion and sin. We didn't belong in His kingdom, let alone His court. But through the blood of Jesus, we have been forgiven, redeemed, and restored. We've been made citizens of the kingdom and more. We've been adopted into the royal family. We are children of the King! "And because we are his children, God has sent the Spirit of his Son into our hearts, prompting us to call out, "Abba, Father" (Galatians 4:6 NLT).

The word *Abba* means "Papa" or "Daddy" . . . it's an intimate, affectionate, familiar name a small child uses for his or her father. Whether your relationship with your earthly father is loving, strained, or even nonexistent, you can run into our heavenly Father's arms for security and comfort, calling Him "Abba" or "Daddy."

As our loving Father, and not just our King, God welcomes us into His presence. He delights in us. He longs for us to come to Him with all of our concerns. He wants us to come when we're happy and excited, when we're worried or afraid, when we're in trouble and we don't know what to do. As our Father, He is in a unique position to help us. He loves us more than anyone else could ever love us. So much that He was willing to give up everything for us—even Jesus, His Son. "See what great love the Father has lavished on us" (1 John 3:1).

He knows us better than we know ourselves. He understands exactly where we are and how we got there and where we need to go from here. He is ready and willing and able to provide all that we need. And so much more! "Let us then approach God's throne of grace with confidence, so that we may receive mercy and find grace to help us in our time of need" (Hebrews 4:16).

Don't hang back in an outer courtyard, or worse yet, relegate

yourself to a position outside the castle walls. That's not where
you belong. Don't keep your distance—like a stranger, a visitor
to the King's court.

Run toward your heavenly Father with full speed. Hurl *why don't we run to God in trusting abandon like a small child?*
yourself into His open arms. Feel His love surround you, His
peace enfold You, and His joy overwhelm you today.

REFLECT

**What is keeping you from running into your heavenly Father's
arms today?** *Feelings that I need to be able to right the wrongs of move forward in this life not being dependent on anyone or anything.*

PRAY

*Lord Jesus, I'm so grateful that through You I have access to the Father.
I am no longer a foreigner, an alien, an outsider. I'm a citizen of Your
kingdom, with all the rights and privileges that citizenship entails. I'm one
of Your chosen people, and more than that, a member of Your family.*

Thank You for inviting me and welcoming me into Your presence with arms open wide. Help me always to come to You and share with You all that is on my heart and mind. Father, I know that You love me and that You care about everything that concerns me today.

OUR HEARTS ARE WHERE GOD'S **HOME IS**

> ❝ *In him the whole building is joined together and rises to become a holy temple in the Lord. And in him you too are being built together to become a dwelling in which God lives by his Spirit.* ❞

—Ephesians 2:21–22

God's people once spent an extraordinary amount of time, effort, and resources to build Him an elaborate and breathtakingly beautiful temple. The kind of temple that kings and queens would travel thousands of miles to see. The kind of temple that would inspire the awe and reverence and worship that God was due. They wanted to bring glory and honor to Him.

But Acts 17:24 tells us, "The God who made the world and everything in it is the Lord of heaven and earth and does not live in temples built by human hands." God is building His own temple, a living temple, in which He dwells: "Don't you know that you yourselves are God's temple and that God's Spirit dwells in your midst?" (1 Corinthians 3:16).

That's right. We are His temple—you and me.

In the first message the apostle Peter preached after the death and resurrection of Jesus, he quoted the words of the prophet Joel to explain the coming of the Holy Spirit: "In the last days, God says, I will pour out my Spirit on all people" (Acts 2:17). In the past, God's Spirit came upon only a handful of men and women who were specially chosen by Him to accomplish a specific task. But today, says Peter, God's Spirit lives in and through all believers, empowering all of us to live a life that honors Him.

Of course, this awesome privilege comes with great responsibility. "Do you not know that your bodies are temples of the Holy Spirit, who is in you, whom you have received from God? You are not your own; you were bought at a price. Therefore honor God with your bodies" (1 Corinthians 6:19–20).

Our salvation cost Jesus dearly—He purchased us with His own blood. So out of gratitude to Him, out of love for Him, we choose to honor His commandments and obey His Word. We choose to do the things we know will please Him, things that will bring glory and honor to Him. We choose not to do the things we know will grieve Him, disappoint Him, dishonor Him, or disrespect Him.

The reward is that we experience the presence of God in amazing, incredibly personal, and powerful ways. Jesus said,

"Anyone who loves me will obey my teaching. My Father will love them, and we will come to them and make our home with them" (John 14:23–24).

Our hearts are His home.

Hallelujah!

REFLECT

What are you doing to take care of your temple today—physically and spiritually? *Working on staying physically fit so that I can go forward in whatever he asks. Having friends help keep me accountable to pursue my spiritual walk.*

PRAY

Lord Jesus, I'm honored to be a holy temple, a dwelling place in which—by Your Spirit—You live. Cleanse me, purify me, and strengthen me. Help me to guard against anything that might corrupt or damage or destroy my temple. Teach me how to care for it, cherish it, and protect it.

I want You to feel welcome, to make Your home in my heart and stay with me forever.

AMAZING **GRACE**

> 66 *I became a servant of this gospel by the gift of God's grace given me through the working of his power. Although I am less than the least of all the Lord's people, this grace was given me.* 99

—Ephesians 3:7–8

*A*mazing. It's the only way to describe the incredible transformation that took place in the life of John Newton. A slave trader in the 1700s, Newton lived a life of drunkenness, profanity, and immorality. He was a foul, ill-tempered man, despised by everyone who knew him. He cared for no one but himself and sought nothing but his own pleasure. When he became captain of his own slave-trading ship, his hard heart grew even harder.

Then one night, John's ship was caught in a fierce storm. He came face-to-face with a gripping fear of death. An experienced sailor, he knew he had little chance of survival and was not ready to face eternity.

John tried to cry out to God for mercy, but he was stopped abruptly by the thought of how little he deserved it. During a harrowing night of soul-searching, he realized that he was a sinner in need of a Savior. He began to understand the meaning of God's grace. Newton survived the storm that night, but he was never the same again. He was a new man.

At the age of thirty-nine, the former slave trader became a pastor. He dedicated the rest of his life to sharing with others the good news of the gospel: that Jesus Christ had come to "seek and to save the lost" (Luke 19:10). Reflecting on his experience that night in the storm, Newton later penned the words that have touched the hearts of millions:

Amazing grace—how sweet the sound
that saved a wretch like me!
I once was lost but now am found,
was blind but now I see.

Through many dangers, toils and snares,
I have already come;
'Tis grace hath brought me safe thus far,
and grace will lead me home.

Throughout his lifetime, Newton never lost sight of the miracle of his salvation. He never ceased to wonder at what God had done in him and through him.

Do we live in a state of wonder of what has been done for us?

Brothers and sisters, think of what you were when you were called. Not many of you were wise by human standards; not many were influential; not many were of noble birth. But God chose the foolish things of the world to shame the wise; God chose the weak things of the world to shame the strong. God chose the lowly things of this world and the despised things—and the things that are not—to nullify the things that are, so that no one may boast before him. It is because of him that you are in Christ Jesus, who has become for us wisdom from God—that is, our righteousness, holiness and redemption. Therefore, as it is written: "Let the one who boasts boast in the Lord." (1 Corinthians 1:26–31)

Boast in the Lord. Newton did!

Praise God, that same grace that John Newton experienced is available for you and me today.

REFLECT

In what ways do you see God's grace at work in your own life today? *FORGIVES ME WHEN I BECOME CONTROLLING & NOT SENSITIVE TO OTHERS; WHEN I LOOK FOR OTHER THINGS & WAYS TO GET ANSWERS TO MY LONGINGS; WHEN I BUSY MYSELF IN A WAY THAT I MISS HIM.*

PRAY

God, I am a servant of the gospel—Your servant—because of Your mercy, grace, and life-transforming power. In my own flesh, in my sin nature, there is nothing of any value or virtue. Nothing worthy of Your love, nothing deserving of Your mercy and grace.

But You have made me worthy through the precious blood of Jesus, Your Son. You have lavished Your love on me. You have saved me, redeemed me, and restored me through Your amazing grace.

FROM THE **BEGINNING**

> ❝ *His intent was that now, through the church, the manifold wisdom of God should be made known to the rulers and authorities in the heavenly realms, according to his eternal purpose which he accomplished in Christ Jesus our Lord.* ❞

—Ephesians 3:10–11

God is eternal. He has always been. He will always be. At some point thousands of years ago, He decided to create the heavens and the earth—the universe as we know it, with all the galaxies, all the stars and planets hurtling through time and space. He created supernatural beings called angels to fill the heavens.

God wanted to show His glory and majesty and wisdom and power. He wanted to share His boundless love. So He created Adam and Eve—the first man and first woman—and gave them a beautiful home in the garden of Eden, a lush paradise of perfection. God told Adam and Eve to "rule over the fish in the sea and the birds in the sky and over every living creature that moves on the ground"—the animals with whom they shared the earth (Genesis 1:28). He gave them the responsibility to care for their garden.

God also gave Adam and Eve free will—the ability to think and choose for themselves what they would do, the ability to give and receive love freely. There was only one rule—one tree whose fruit they weren't supposed to touch. But even one rule was too much for Adam and Eve to follow. They were easily tempted and led astray. For they were not alone in the garden.

Earlier there had been a rebellion in heaven. One of the archangels, Lucifer, had sought God's power and glory for himself. God cast him out of heaven and made it clear that his ultimate judgment, his final punishment, was still to come. But until such time as God saw fit to end it, they would be engaged in a mighty battle of epic proportions.

Though he was powerless to take on God Himself in all His glory, Lucifer saw an opportunity to hurt God—to wound His heart—by destroying the beauty of His creation and turning His precious children against Him. Lucifer found that he could fill Adam and Eve with greed and pride and rebellion, to spur them on to defiance and disobedience. He appeared as a serpent in the garden of Eden and tempted Eve to eat the forbidden fruit. Eve gave the fruit to Adam, and their innocence was lost. So was their sweet fellowship with God—the precious relationship they had enjoyed with Him in the garden. To protect them, God cast them out of Eden. Adam and Eve and all of their descendants were sentenced to struggle and labor and pain—and eventually to face old age and death, instead of eternal youth and life.

God was not caught off guard by this turn of events. He knew all along that given a choice, this is what the human heart would choose. But so great was His mercy and love that from the beginning He had made a way to set things right. He put a plan in motion to rescue the human race. As He sent them out of Eden, God told Adam and Eve that He would undo the damage they had done. One of their descendants would do what they had not been able to do: obey. Through His obedience, He would save humankind. And He would crush the serpent forever.

> He forgave us all our sins, having canceled the charge of our legal indebtedness, which stood against us and condemned us; he has taken it away, nailing it to the cross. And having disarmed the powers and authorities, he made a public spectacle of them, triumphing over them by the cross. (Colossians 2:13–15)

Mission accomplished.

REFLECT

How does this eternal perspective—seeing God's sovereignty through the ages—affect your heart and life today?

Makes me wonder why I think I can do any of my life on my own. We are all so prone to stray. We can't make it on our own doing.

PRAY

Father God, through the church, Your great wisdom has been made known to the rulers and authorities in the heavenly realms, according to Your eternal purpose that You accomplished in Christ Jesus our Lord. You do everything that You purpose to do; nothing can disrupt or derail Your plans. My life is in Your hands.

A SACRED **SACRIFICE**

 66 *I ask you, therefore, not to be discouraged because of
my sufferings for you, which are your glory.* 99

—Ephesians 3:13

To us, salvation is free. We don't have to earn it or achieve it.
We just receive it. We believe it. But our salvation cost Jesus everything. And often, it has cost His followers everything to
share it with others. Most of the first disciples died martyrs' deaths.
Since then, countless preachers, teachers, missionaries, Bible trans-
lators, and everyday Christians have faced suffering, persecution,
and even death simply for holding out the hope of the gospel and
holding on to the truth they received. Of these martyrs, the Bible
says, "the world was not worthy of them" (Hebrews 11:38).

Jesus said we shouldn't be discouraged when we learn of
Christians who are suffering—or when we experience it ourselves. It doesn't mean that God has abandoned us or failed us—
or that we have somehow failed Him. Suffering is a very real
part of the life He's called us to. Jesus said, "In this world you

will have trouble. But take heart! I have overcome the world" (John 16:33).

Like those who have gone before us, we, too, may one day be called—if we haven't been already—to risk, to struggle, to sacrifice, and to suffer for the gospel of Jesus Christ. But this isn't something to fear. It's something to celebrate!

> Consider it pure joy, my brothers and sisters, whenever you face trials of many kinds, because you know that the testing of your faith produces perseverance. . . . Blessed is the one who perseveres under trial because, having stood the test, that person will receive the crown of life that the Lord has promised to those who love him. (James 1:2–3, 12)

The apostle Paul said, "I rejoice in what I am suffering for you" (Colossians 1:24). Paul understood—and wanted us to know—that it is such an enormous honor, such a great privilege to be Christ's witnesses, to lead others to faith in Jesus and to bring them into the family of God. Forever.

> Therefore we do not lose heart. Though outwardly we are wasting away, yet inwardly we are being renewed day by day. For our light and momentary troubles are achieving for us an eternal glory that far outweighs them all. So we fix our eyes not on what is seen, but on what

is unseen, since what is seen is temporary, but what is unseen is eternal. (2 Corinthians 4:16–18)

When we focus on our eternal hope, the eternal glory, our earthly pain loses its power and significance. It can be gladly endured for the joy that can never be shaken.

REFLECT

Has it cost you anything yet to be a follower of Jesus Christ? Have you suffered or sacrificed anything for Him?

It's cost me some friendships & dates.

PRAY

Lord Jesus, thank You for the people who have been willing to suffer and sacrifice to bring the gospel to me. Thank You for the men and women who through the ages have been willing to give everything so that I might hear Your Word, know Your truth, and live strong in Your love. Thank You for the people in my own life who have taken risks and made sacrifices to be able to share Your salvation with me.

Let me not be discouraged by the thought of suffering—theirs or my own.
Make me willing to give my all for You. May I be bold, courageous,
determined, generous, and selfless as I share with others today.
Teach me to count it all joy and persevere through every trial,
for Your glory. Amen.

A CREDIT TO THE **NAME**

For this reason I kneel before the Father, from whom every family in heaven and on earth derives its name.

—Ephesians 3:14–15

Have you ever seen those *Supernanny* or *Nanny 911* TV shows? You know, where a woman with a lot of experience working with children and families brings order to a household wildly out of control?

Sometimes when you see how atrociously the kids on these shows behave, you can't help but think, *What is wrong with their parents? Why don't they do something about this?*

You know, sometimes the way we as Christians behave has the world asking the same thing about our heavenly Father. See, the way we behave—the way we live our lives—is a profound reflection of our faith. It says something not only about who we are, but about what we believe and who we believe in. In a very real sense, it's God's name—it's His reputation—at stake.

Think about it: When His children are unruly, rebellious, and out of control, it brings shame on Him (Titus 2:6–15, 3:1–2). What kind of Father is He, anyway? And the world says, "If His own children won't obey Him—if they don't respect Him, why should we?" They have a point.

And we have no excuse.

> For the grace of God has appeared that offers salvation to all people. It teaches us to say "No" to ungodliness and worldly passions, and to live self-controlled, upright and godly lives in this present age, while we wait for the blessed hope—the appearing of the glory of our great God and Savior, Jesus Christ, who gave himself for us to redeem us from all wickedness and to purify for himself a people that are his very own, eager to do what is good. (Titus 2:11–14)

When the grace of God can be seen at work in His children—when they are self-controlled, godly, upright people who are "eager to do what is good"—they bring glory and honor to His name. The world sees something they are compelled to admire and respect. And ultimately, more people find their way home to Him.

So the next time you're tempted to ignore the house rules, pick a fight with your brothers and sisters in Christ, throw a tantrum, or act out—think twice. Remember, it isn't only God who's watching. It isn't only Him—or you—who will be hurt.

Choose instead to do what you know is right. Set a good example. Be the kind of child a Father—and the whole family of God—can be proud of!

REFLECT

Think about the challenges you face today—the tasks, the circumstances, and the relationships. What can you do to handle these challenges in a way that reflects positively on your heavenly Father and the family that bears His name?

PRAY

Father, I kneel before You and ask Your forgiveness for the times I have brought dishonor or discredit to Your name. You are so loving, so merciful, so patient, so kind. I want to live my life in such a way that I can bring glory and honor to Your name. I want to encourage and inspire my brothers and sisters to do the same. May our lives be such a witness to Your transforming love, Your life-changing power, that others want to become part of Your family too.

INSIDE **OUT**

> ❝ *I pray that out of his glorious riches he may strengthen you with power through his Spirit in your inner being, so that Christ may dwell in your hearts through faith.* ❞

—Ephesians 3:16–17

D o you ever feel intimidated by other people? Outshined, overshadowed, insignificant?

Experts have all kinds of suggestions for how you might boost your confidence and self-esteem: they say you begin by practicing positive self-talk or attending an assertiveness training seminar. But I think there's a solution that goes a lot deeper and lasts a lot longer than any self-help steps to success.

It starts with having a biblical understanding of who God created you to be, what He created you for, and why you are so precious to Him. "People look at the outward appearance, but the LORD looks at the heart" (1 Samuel 16:7).

Spend some time meditating on passages of Scripture like Psalm 139, Jeremiah 29:11, or Jeremiah 31:3, in which God says, "I have loved you with an everlasting love." Other passages you may want to study include Ephesians 2:10; 4:22–24; and 1 Peter 2:9. "For you are a people holy to the LORD your God. The LORD your God has chosen you out of all the peoples on the face of the earth to be his people, his treasured possession" (Deuteronomy 7:6).

God calls you His treasure!

> But we have this treasure in jars of clay to show that this all-surpassing power is from God and not from us. We are hard pressed on every side, but not crushed; perplexed, but not in despair; persecuted, but not abandoned; struck down, but not destroyed. . . . Therefore we do not lose heart. Though outwardly we are wasting away, yet inwardly we are being renewed day by day. For our light and momentary troubles are achieving for us an eternal glory that far outweighs them all. So we fix our eyes not on what is seen, but on what is unseen, since what is seen is temporary, but what is unseen is eternal. (2 Corinthians 4:7–9, 16–18)

Now make a point of spending time on your knees in prayer, remembering who God is . . . how awesome, how mighty, how powerful, how majestic. All of creation bows before Him, and the kings of the earth get their power from Him and will one day answer to Him.

> For in him all things were created: things in heaven and on earth, visible and invisible, whether thrones or powers or rulers or authorities; all things have been created through him and for him. He is before all things, and in him all things hold together. (Colossians 1:16–17)

He is the King of kings and the Lord of lords. The Most High God. And you are His servant (Acts 2:18) and His child (1 John 3:1). But more than that—He calls you His friend (John 15:15).

Puts things into perspective, doesn't it?

That's why a wise yet anonymous saint once observed, "He who kneels before God can stand before anyone!"

REFLECT

Are you stronger on the outside or the inside? In other words, is your confidence just "putting on a brave face" or do you *know* you are living strong in His strength today?

PRAY

God, out of Your glorious riches, strengthen me with power through Your Spirit in my inner being, so that Christ may dwell in my heart through faith. May my confidence, my peace, my joy, my trust, and my faith be found in You. Remind me that You see my heart and that's what really counts. I want to be holy and pleasing to You.

LOVE, TRUE **LOVE**

> ❝ *And I pray that you, being rooted and established in love, may have power, together with all the Lord's holy people, to grasp how wide and long and high and deep is the love of Christ.* ❞

—Ephesians 3:17–18

Love is one of the greatest longings of the human heart. Some would say *the* greatest longing is to love and be loved. But what does that mean? What does it look like? How does it feel? Is what we've experienced the real thing—and is it all there is? Or is there something more?

The Bible gives us a beautiful description of love—true love—in 1 Corinthians 13:

Love is patient, love is kind. It does not envy, it does not boast, it is not proud. It does not dishonor others, it is not self-seeking, it is not easily angered, it keeps no record of wrongs. Love does not delight in evil but rejoices with the truth. It always protects, always trusts, always hopes, always perseveres. Love never fails. (vv. 4–8)

We don't have to wonder; we can know what true love is—what it looks like and feels like—what it means to truly love someone and to be truly loved by them in return.

But wait! There's more . . .

The Bible tells us, "This is how God showed his love among us: He sent his one and only Son into the world that we might live through him. This is love: not that we loved God, but that he loved us and sent his Son as an atoning sacrifice for our sins" (1 John 4:9–10).

In case you missed it: "This is how we know what love is: Jesus Christ laid down his life for us" (1 John 3:16).

The ultimate example of committed, sacrificial love is Jesus Himself. The Scripture says, "Greater love has no one than this: to lay down one's life for one's friends" (John 15:13). And that's just what Jesus did for us.

See, you *do* know what it means to be loved—truly loved. Please share that love with someone else today.

The love of God is greater far
Than tongue or pen can ever tell;
It goes beyond the highest star,
And reaches to the lowest hell;

The guilty pair, bowed down with care,
God gave His Son to win;
His erring child He reconciled,
And pardoned from his sin.
—Frederick M. Lehman

REFLECT

**Who do you know who needs to experience the love of Jesus?
Who could you share with today?**

PRAY

*Lord, You loved me long before I ever loved You. You sent Your only Son
to die for me. This kind of love is beyond my comprehension. Now as I'm
being rooted and established in Your love, as I grow in my knowledge
and experience and understanding of You, please give me the power,
together with all my brothers and sisters in Christ, to grasp how wide
and long and high and deep is Your love for me. Help me to know
Your love, to share Your love, and to live strong in Your love.*

I WANT TO KNOW WHAT **LOVE** IS

> 66 *... and to know this love that surpasses knowledge— that you may be filled to the measure of all the fullness of God.* 99

—Ephesians 3:19

Paul prays that we will "know" the love God has for us, that we will really grasp this life-transforming truth. The kind of knowing he prays for isn't just "head knowledge"—an intellectual assent to an established fact. It's "heart knowledge"—an ever-expanding, deepening, growing comprehension of a reality that cannot be fully understood apart from the supernatural intervention of God.

The Amplified Bible translates Ephesians 3:19 this way:

[That you may really come] to know [practically, through experience for yourselves] the love of Christ, which far surpasses mere knowledge [without experience]; that you may be filled [through all your being] unto all the fullness of God [may have the richest measure of the divine Presence, and become a body wholly filled and flooded with God Himself]!

This is what Jesus is talking about when He says, "I have come that they may have life, and have it to the full" (John 10:10). Truly knowing Jesus, knowing His love, and knowing His truth comes from experiencing Him. Meeting Him often in the pages of His Word.

The psalmist prayed, "Show me your ways, LORD, teach me your paths. Guide me in your truth and teach me, for you are God my Savior, and my hope is in you all day long" (Psalm 25:4–5).

Truly knowing Jesus comes from trusting Him, believing Him, and obeying Him. Putting His teachings into practice. Watching Him actively work in our lives and the lives of those around us—over time and in an abundance of circumstances.

This is how Paul could say, "I know whom I have believed, and am convinced that he is able to guard what I have entrusted to him until that day" (2 Timothy 1:12). It's how John could say, "We know how much God loves us, and we have put our trust in his love" (1 John 4:16 NLT).

In Romans 8:38–39, Paul added, "I am convinced that neither death nor life, neither angels nor demons, neither the present nor the future, nor any powers, neither height nor depth, nor anything else in all creation, will be able to separate us from the love of God that is in Christ Jesus our Lord."

That's the love God has for us.

REFLECT

If someone asked you, how would you say you have personally, practically, through your own experience—come to know the love of Christ? *I have seen Him make things happen that humanly we or I couldn't make happen - Plans coming together at southside, Dad coming back, giving me a word to say to someone at just the time they need it. Having things given to me that I wasn't expecting.*

PRAY

Lord, teach me to know—to truly comprehend, to understand at the deepest level of my being—the love You have for me. A love that will not let me go and will never be taken from me. Help me to recognize it, receive it, and experience it in a real, practical, and uniquely personal way.

Fill me with Your Holy Spirit. Flood my whole being with Your divine presence, all the fullness of God, that I might know You deeply, love You completely, serve You faithfully, and share You freely with all who come my way.

PAUL'S **DOXOLOGY**

> " *Now to him who is able to do immeasurably more than all we ask or imagine, according to his power that is at work within us.* "

—Ephesians 3:20

Have you ever been so amazed by God, so in awe of who He is and what He has done, that you burst into spontaneous praise? If you haven't, or haven't recently, it may be that you've been taking Him for granted. Perhaps you've just been going through the motions lately. Maybe the trials and tribulations of life have distracted you.

We have so much to praise God for, even in the simplest, most basic truths of our faith. The joy of our salvation, the peace that comes from knowing our sins are forgiven. The hope of heaven and eternal life.

In the book of Romans, the apostle Paul was writing to the early church, explaining God's plan of salvation through Jesus Christ, His Son. As he contemplated the infinite wisdom of the God who had established this plan before He even laid the foundations of the earth—as he realized the mercy of God, the lengths to which God had gone to reconcile Himself to man, and the provision He had made for all people—Paul's excitement grew.

Finally, he couldn't contain himself. Paul interrupted his dissertation to exclaim,

Oh, the depth of the riches of the wisdom and knowledge of God! How unsearchable his judgments, and his paths beyond tracing out! "Who has known the mind of the Lord? Or who has been his counselor? Who has ever given to God, that God should repay them?" For from him and through him and to him are all things. To him be the glory forever! Amen. (Romans 11:33–36)

Not long afterward, Paul wrote a letter to the believers in Ephesus. He was praying that God would open the eyes of their hearts, to help them truly know and rely on the love God has for us, to experience that love in all its depth and life-transforming power. He ended his prayer with another beautiful doxology—a hymn, an outpouring of praise from his heart to God's:

Now to him who is able to do immeasurably more than all we ask or imagine, according to his power that is at work within us, to him be glory in the church and in Christ Jesus throughout all generations, for ever and ever! Amen. (Ephesians 3:20–21)

How incredible, how amazing it is to know that our hearts are held by One who loves us deeply, pursues us passionately, protects and provides for us faithfully, and can do more in us and through us and for us than we could ever ask or even imagine!

REFLECT

If you were to pour out your heart to God right now, what words of praise would fill your tongue?

What would you thank Him for? What would you ask Him for? *LIFE, HEALTH, FRIENDS, RESOURCES, HIS PATIENCE, HIS LONG-SUFFERING ON MY BEHALF, THE FREEDOM TO WORSHIP HIM. PARENTS WHO SAW TO IT THAT I WAS INTRODUCED TO YOU EARLY ON & SURROUNDED ME W/PEOPLE ALONG THE WAY WHO LOVED ME & GREW ME UP.*

PRAY

Lord, my heart is full of love for You. I could never praise You or thank You enough for Your love, Your life, and Your power working in me and through me. To You, the One who is able to do immeasurably more than all we ask or imagine, according to Your power that is at work within us, be all glory and honor forever and ever. Amen.

TO GOD BE THE **GLORY**

> **“** . . . to him be glory in the church and in Christ Jesus throughout all generations, for ever and ever! Amen. **”**

—Ephesians 3:21

After four hundred years of slavery in Egypt and forty years of wandering in the wilderness, they had finally arrived! As Joshua led the Israelites into the promised land, God did many amazing things to show them that He was with them, that He would bless them in this new land. When the people arrived at the banks of the Jordan River, it was harvesttime—and the river was at its fullest. But as the priests carrying the ark of the covenant stepped into the water at the river's edge, the flow of water miraculously ceased—it was cut off upstream, and all the people crossed the riverbed on dry land.

While the priests stood there, Joshua sent the leaders of the twelve tribes back to the riverbed, commanding each of them to gather a large stone to build a memorial. "In the future," he said, "when your children ask you, 'What do these stones mean?' tell them that the flow of the Jordan was cut off before the ark of the covenant of the LORD. . . . These stones are to be a memorial to the people of Israel forever" (Joshua 4:6–7).

People all over the world still build memorials today. A memorial is a wonderful way to remember something precious, something historic, something important. It's a tradition each of us can carry on in our own hearts, with our own families.

The psalmist exclaimed,

> As for me, I will always have hope; I will praise you more and more. My mouth will tell of your righteous deeds. . . . Since my youth, God, you have taught me, and to this day I declare your marvelous deeds. Even when I am old and gray, do not forsake me, my God, till I declare your power to the next generation, your mighty acts to all who are to come. (Psalm 71:14–18)

When God does something miraculous in your life, take time to build a memorial—to do something special to create a memory of this experience. Write it down in a journal, scrapbook it, sing about it, recreate it, or record it somehow. Tell your friends and family, especially your children and grandchildren. Relive the experience over and over in your heart, so that you'll never forget what the Lord has done for you!

REFLECT

In what specific ways can you give God glory for the things He has done in your life?

How can you pass on your story—God's story—and share His mighty acts with the next generation?

PRAY

God, when I think of all the things You have done—throughout history, throughout my life, in my own story—I'm amazed. Overwhelmed. Speechless. Lord, I stand in awe of You. I can't even begin to love You or serve You or thank You or praise You enough. Show me how I can hold on to the memories and relive the miracles, keep them uppermost in my mind, and share the stories with those who come after me. To You be the glory in the church and in Christ Jesus throughout all generations, for ever and ever! Amen.

THE HALL OF **FAITH**

" *As a prisoner for the Lord, then, I urge you to live a life worthy of the calling you have received.* "

—Ephesians 4:1

Hebrews 11 is sometimes called the "Hall of Faith" chapter of the Bible. It tells the stories of men and women of God down through the ages who put their faith in Him. It was by faith that they "conquered kingdoms, administered justice, and gained what was promised . . . shut the mouths of lions, quenched the fury of the flames, and escaped the edge of the sword" (vv. 33–34).

Their weakness was turned to strength; they became powerful in battle and routed foreign armies.

Women received back their dead, raised to life again. There were others who were tortured, refusing to be released so that they might gain an even better resurrection. Some faced jeers and flogging, and even chains and imprisonment. They were put to death by stoning; they were sawed in two; they were killed by the sword. They went about . . . destitute, persecuted and mistreated—the world was not worthy of them. (vv. 35–38)

The writer of Hebrews notes in this stirring and inspirational chapter, "All these people were still living by faith when they died. They did not receive the things promised; they only saw them and welcomed them from a distance" (v. 13).

In other words, these heroes of the faith didn't get to witness the coming of Jesus, their Messiah, the Holy One of Israel. But we know of it through the Word. They didn't have the privilege of responding to the good news of the gospel, but we do. God "counted their faith as righteousness"[3]—He gave them credit for believing everything He had revealed to them in their own time, and they are now in heaven—"a great cloud of witnesses" cheering us on as we make the journey and run our own "race" of faith![4]

The apostle Paul urged us as believers to be passionate in our pursuit of godliness and spiritual maturity, enthusiastic about tackling all the challenges that come our way. In 1 Corinthians 9:24–25, he said,

Do you not know that in a race all the runners run, but only one gets the prize? Run in such a way as to get the prize. Everyone who competes in the games goes into strict training. They do it to get a crown that will not last, but we do it to get a crown that will last forever.

No matter what challenges we face, no matter how tough it gets, we've got to stay focused if we want to live strong. We've got to keep our eyes on that prize to finish well!

Therefore, since we are surrounded by such a great cloud of witnesses, let us throw off everything that hinders and the sin that so easily entangles. And let us run with perseverance the race marked out for us, fixing our eyes on Jesus, the pioneer and perfecter of faith. (Hebrews 12:1–2)

He is our focal point. Our inspiration. Our motivation. May we live worthy of the calling we, too, have received.

REFLECT

In this season of your life, who or what inspires you most to live a life worthy of your calling?

PRAY

Lord Jesus, help me to live a life worthy of my calling—Your calling on my life. I want to make the most of every opportunity You have given me to bring glory and honor to You.

Make me joyful in hope, patient in affliction, faithful in prayer. Give me the heart to share with Your people who are in need and practice hospitality. Empower me by Your Holy Spirit to overcome any hurt, bitterness, or unforgiveness. Enable me to bless those who persecute me, to rejoice with those who rejoice, and to mourn with those who mourn. Help me live in harmony with my brothers and sisters in Christ. At the end of my days, I long to hear You say, "Well done, good and faithful servant." All the glory will belong to You.

FINDER'S **FEE**

> " *Be completely humble and gentle; be patient,
> bearing with one another in love.* "

—Ephesians 4:2

The other day I ran across a profound expression: "Some people find fault like there was a reward for it!" Sad but true. There are some people who seem to live their lives to find fault with others. It's like they have nothing better to do than to catch other people making mistakes and call them on it.

Well actually, I think there is a reward—a "finder's fee" for this kind of critical attitude and approach to others. When all you see is the bad in people, you get a heavy spirit. And you get a reputation for being a negative person. You get lots of time to yourself, because nobody wants to be around you. And you get God's solemn promise that He will one day hold you to the same impossible standard to which you've held others.

Jesus said:

Do not judge, or you too will be judged. For in the same way you judge others, you will be judged, and with the measure you use, it will be measured to you. Why do you look at the speck of sawdust in your brother's eye and pay no attention to the plank in your own eye? How can you say to your brother, 'Let me take the speck out of your eye,' when all the time there is a plank in your own eye? . . . First take the plank out of your eye, and then you will see clearly to remove the speck from your brother's eye. (Matthew 7:1–5)

There is a reward for finding fault, but I wouldn't recommend collecting it. Instead, be merciful to others—as God is merciful to you. Try looking for the good in people. Encourage their efforts, no matter how small. Stand with them in their fight against sin and temptation, and pick them up when they fall. Build them up, instead of tearing them down.

Isn't this what you would want others to do for you?

Therefore, as God's chosen people, holy and dearly loved, clothe yourselves with compassion, kindness, humility, gentleness and patience. Bear with each other and forgive one another if any of you has a grievance against someone. Forgive as the Lord forgave you. And over all these virtues put on love, which binds them all together in perfect unity. (Colossians 3:12–14)

When you do these things, you'll find your own spirit will soar, and you'll collect a much better reward!

REFLECT

Which is your greatest challenge: being humble, being gentle, being patient, or bearing with others?

How can you line up your attitudes and behaviors with God's Word?

PRAY

Lord Jesus, I confess that too often I'm quick to find fault with the people around me—in my family or my church family, in my workplace or in my school, neighborhood, and community. Forgive me for being self-righteous, critical, and judgmental of others' weaknesses.

Change my heart, God. Make me humble, gentle, patient, and kind.

Help me bear with others, help me be compassionate and forgiving, giving others the benefit of the doubt. Help me treat others the way I want to be treated—the way You treat me. Let me be a true reflection of Your amazing, unfailing, unconditional love.

WE ARE **ONE**

66 *Make every effort to keep the unity of the Spirit through the bond of peace. There is one body and one Spirit, just as you were called to one hope when you were called; one Lord, one faith, one baptism; one God and Father of all, who is over all and through all and in all.* 99

—Ephesians 4:3-6

Every time Tino Wallenda-Zoppe goes to work, he puts his life on the line—literally! Zoppe is a member of the world-renowned tightrope walkers The Flying Wallendas. Thirty feet above ground, and without a net, this circus performer faces the ultimate test of concentration and skill almost every day. One trademark routine features Tino riding across the wire on a bicycle while his daughter Alida stands on his shoulders. His wife, Olinka, hangs below him on a trapeze, balancing on her head. It's breathtaking—and very dangerous.

"Everybody has to coordinate their balance with everyone else," Tino explains. "If somebody makes a false move, it can cause everybody to lose their balance."[5]

You know, the same is true for us in the family of God. We were created to function as a unit—the body of Christ.

It is important to understand that when the Bible talks about unity, it means "being like-minded, having the same love, being one in spirit and of one mind" (Philippians 2:2). Unity is not the same thing as uniformity—a loss of individuality, the absence of any healthy difference or debate. On the contrary! "As iron sharpens iron, so one person sharpens another" (Proverbs 27:17). The Scripture is clear that God intended each of us to be unique and individual. He gave us different personalities, different experiences and perspectives, different gifts and talents, different roles and responsibilities. At its best, all this diversity actually facilitates and strengthens our unity.

Each of us has our own vital and necessary role to play. In 1 Corinthians 12, we're told:

> The eye cannot say to the hand, 'I don't need you!' And the head cannot say to the feet, 'I don't need you!' . . . There should be no division in the body, but that its parts should have equal concern for each other. If one part suffers, every part suffers with it. (vv. 21, 25–26)

When one of us stumbles and falls, we all get hurt.

In order to keep our balance in our Christian walk, we must strengthen one another, support one another, and work together to accomplish God's purposes. Scripture reminds us to "encourage one another and build each other up" (1 Thessalonians 5:11). Hebrews 10:24 says, "Let us consider how we may spur one another on toward love and good deeds."

Working together, we'll all make it safely—and triumphantly—to eternity with our Lord!

REFLECT

What can you personally do to promote unity in your family or your church family—the body of Christ—today?

PRAY

You have made us one body and one spirit. You have called us to one hope through one Lord, one faith, one baptism, one God and Father of all. The differences in our cultures, our backgrounds, our gifts and talents, our personalities, and our experiences should only enrich us, not divide us. We need each other in order to live strong for You.

Help us make every effort to keep the unity of the Spirit that You have given us—to treasure it, to preserve it, to protect it, and promote it. Teach me to love and respect and appreciate all of my brothers and sisters in Christ and live with them in peace.

FILET OF **PASTOR**

> **❝** *So Christ himself gave the apostles, the prophets, the evangelists, the pastors and teachers, to equip his people for works of service, so that the body of Christ may be built up until we all reach unity in the faith and in the knowledge of the Son of God and become mature, attaining to the whole measure of the fullness of Christ.* **❞**

—Ephesians 4:11–13

In a sketch called "Sunday Dinner," humorist Martha Bolton describes a typical Christian family, sitting down for a meal at a fancy French restaurant. The menu offers some rather unusual entrees, such as Filet of Pastor, Church Treasurer Florentine, Leg o' Youth Pastor, Evangelist Kabobs, and Deacon DeJour.[6]

This is Bolton's witty way of drawing attention to the fact that many Christians choose not to obey the biblical admonition to honor those in authority over us:

Remember your leaders who taught you the word of

God. Think of all the good that has come from their lives, and follow the example of their faith. . . . Obey your spiritual leaders, and do what they say. Their work is to watch over your souls, and they are accountable to God. Give them reason to do this with joy and not with sorrow. (Hebrews 13:7, 17 NLT)

Instead we make a habit of indulging in gossip and backbiting. We routinely critique the Sunday service and criticize those responsible for leading it.

It's true that we are supposed to "test the spirits" (1 John 4:1) and carefully evaluate the teaching we receive in light of God's Word. Church leaders are not infallible, above the law, or exempt from godly correction and discipline. They are, after all, human beings—frail and flawed, just like us.

But 1 Timothy 5:17 clearly states that those "who direct the affairs of the church well are worthy of double honor, especially those whose work is preaching and teaching."

God has given these precious people to us to teach us His Word, to help us apply it to our lives, and to enable us to grow in our faith and maturity. They have a tremendous amount of responsibility. God holds them to a higher standard. "Not many of you should become teachers, my fellow believers, because you know that we who teach will be judged more strictly" (James 3:1).

These leaders make many sacrifices for the sake of the

ministry. They need our support. They deserve our love and respect. They don't need endless criticism, petty conflicts, and constant complaints.

The next time you sit down to a Sunday dinner, pass on the filet of church staff—and choose instead conversation that is edifying and uplifting. It's so much more satisfying!

REFLECT

What are some specific ways you can show your appreciation for those who minister to you and to your church family?

PRAY

God, thank You for those You have called as apostles, prophets, evangelists, pastors, and teachers. You have anointed and empowered them to prepare us for Your kingdom work, building up the body of Christ until we all reach unity in the faith and in the knowledge of Your Son. Bless them, strengthen them, and encourage them. Protect them and provide for them. Guide them with Your wisdom.

Enfold them in Your love.

Help us to appreciate, support, encourage, and lift each other up, so that together we may become spiritually mature, attaining the whole measure of the fullness of Christ. In Your precious name, amen.

READ IT **YOURSELF!**

> 66 *Then we will no longer be infants, tossed back and forth by the waves, and blown here and there by every wind of teaching and by the cunning and craftiness of people in their deceitful scheming. Instead, speaking the truth in love, we will grow to become in every respect the mature body of him who is the head, that is, Christ.* 99

—Ephesians 4:14–15

You know, some of us have learned everything we know about our faith from someone else—a pastor, a Sunday school teacher, or a Christian radio program. But we've never actually studied the Bible for ourselves. Unfortunately, our lack of firsthand knowledge of the Word of God puts us at a real disadvantage when it comes to living out the faith we profess.

For one thing, we miss out on the joy of personal discovery—the thrill when, through the Scriptures, God speaks directly to us. We find we lack the confidence to share our beliefs and convictions, because we can't back them up with Scripture.

We're not *exactly* sure what the Bible says and where it says so. Worst of all, when we're content to take somebody else's word for it, we leave ourselves wide open to false doctrine—faulty or misleading teachings. We're as helpless as babies, as hapless as a little boat tossed on the waves, or a leaf blowing in the wind.

Acts 17:11 tells us that the Berean people had a much different approach: When Paul came, preaching the gospel of Jesus Christ, they listened to his message "with great eagerness." Then, they "examined the Scriptures every day to see if what Paul said was true." Because they studied the Word for themselves, they were able to recognize and discern the truth of the gospel message, and they received it with great joy.

Their diligence sets a great example for all of us who are believers. "Do your best to present yourself to God as one approved, a worker who does not need to be ashamed and who correctly handles the word of truth" (2 Timothy 2:15).

If you haven't made personal Bible study a regular part of your daily life, I encourage you to start today.

All Scripture is inspired by God and is useful to teach us what is true and to make us realize what is wrong in our lives. It corrects us when we are wrong and teaches us to do what is right. God uses it to prepare and equip his people to do every good work. (2 Timothy 3:16–17 NLT)

It's time you explored the treasures of God's Word for yourself. You'll be glad you did!

REFLECT

In what ways are you actively filling your heart and mind with God's truth today?

PRAY

Father God, when it comes to discerning Your truth, I don't want to be helpless and hapless, tossed back and forth, blown here and there by every wind of teaching. Don't let me fall victim to the schemes of crafty and cunning deceivers who twist the Scriptures to serve their own agenda, who pervert the truth for their own gain. Protect me from them. Fill me with Your knowledge, wisdom, and truth. Help me to read and understand Your Word. Help me to meditate on it until it becomes a part of me. Speaking the truth in love—calmly, wisely, graciously—my fellow believers and I will grow in our spiritual maturity, becoming more and more like Jesus—the head of the body. Amen.

OUT WITH THE **OLD**; IN WITH THE **NEW**

> ❝ You were taught, with regard to your former way of life, to put off your old self, which is being corrupted by its deceitful desires; to be made new in the attitude of your minds; and to put on the new self, created to be like God in true righteousness and holiness. ❞

—Ephesians 4:22–24

Years ago, a preacher walked the streets of a desperately wicked city. Night and day, he called the people to repent. Boldly, and with a loud voice, he listed the many sins they had committed against God. He made it clear, in no uncertain terms, what was wrong with their behavior—how it failed to meet God's standards, and what kind of life God had called them to. He quoted the Scripture and expounded on its meaning and application to the people around him.

Overwhelmingly, the response to the preacher was ridicule and derision. Some people smirked as they walked past; others snarled. At times they were verbally and even physically abusive. Yet the man of God was undeterred. Day after day, year after year, he preached until he was hoarse—without any apparent success. Not a single convert. And certainly no citywide revival.

One day an arrogant young man sauntered up to the preacher and sneered, "Why don't you give up, you old fool? Can't you see it's useless? You're never going to change them!"

"I'm not preaching to change them," the man replied. "I'm preaching so they don't change me."

Today we live in a world that is increasingly hostile to our faith—a culture that exalts every kind of evil and immorality. A culture that is hell-bent on conforming us to its values, either by force or by seduction. And unfortunately, it has the help of our old nature—our own sinful desires! A little compromise here, a little compromise there. Before we know it, we have slid right into an attitude, an outlook, a way of life that looks nothing like the kind of life that God has called us to. A life of righteousness. A life of holiness.

In 1 Peter 1:14–16, we read:

You must live as God's obedient children. Don't slip back into your old ways of living to satisfy your own desires. You didn't know any better then. But now you must be holy in everything you do, just as God who chose you is holy. For the Scriptures say, "You must be holy because I am holy." (NLT)

"Holy" means set apart as special or sacred. Noble, virtuous, and true. It describes God and those who are devoted or dedicated to Him. Those who belong to Him and to whom He belongs.

Why would we trade this precious privilege for anything the world has to offer, anything we once left behind?

REFLECT

In what ways do you feel the pressure and influence of the culture around you?

How are you affected by the culture?

PRAY

Lord, You have taught me to let go of my old life—my sinful life— which is corrupted and contaminated by its sinful desires. You are making me new in the attitude of my mind, helping me put on my new self, the "me" created to be like You in true righteousness and holiness.

Help me to do my part to guard my heart, to be careful about the things and the people I expose it to. Don't let me fall back into my old ways, compromised by the culture I live or work in. Keep me living strong and growing in righteousness, in holiness, in Christlikeness day by day.

A BATH IN **WRATH**

> ❝ *"In your anger do not sin": Do not let the sun go down while you are still angry, and do not give the devil a foothold.* ❞

—Ephesians 4:26–27

Being angry isn't a sin. Sometimes God is angry. During His earthly ministry, Jesus became angry, outraged, by hypocrisy, by dishonesty, by wickedness, evil, and oppression. But He was without sin. Yet for us, anger often leads to sin. When our emotions boil over, we don't think clearly. We tend to make poor choices, to do or say things that are harmful to ourselves as well as to others. Even if we keep it inside—*especially* if we keep it inside—the damage can be devastating.

Author and speaker Patsy Clairmont says, "I confess I have sometimes taken a bath in wrath. I've soaked in it, lathered up with it, and then splashed around in it. I've lingered in it for days, months, and even years. The result is not unlike sitting in a tub too long—we shrivel up."[7]

Unrighteous, uncontrolled anger is dangerous to our spirits, our hearts, and our minds. It gets a hold on us and won't let go. That's why the Scriptures urge us not to allow ourselves to get angry in the first place: "Refrain from anger and turn from wrath; do not fret—it leads only to evil" (Psalm 37:8). We learn that "everyone should be quick to listen, slow to speak and slow to become angry, because human anger does not produce the righteousness that God desires" (James 1:19–20).

God wants us to have self-control and to make good, wise, and God-honoring choices. As believers, we are not called to a life of anger, bitterness, and hate. We are called to live a life of love. "Love is patient, love is kind. It does not envy, it does not boast, it is not proud. It does not dishonor others, . . . it is not easily angered, it keeps no record of wrongs" (1 Corinthians 13:4–5).

Even when we can't help being angry, when it seems we have good reasons—maybe even righteous reasons—we need to focus our energy on fixing the problem, in our hearts or in our circumstances. We need to right the wrong, resolve the misunderstanding, communicate more clearly, set boundaries when necessary, apologize for our part, and be willing to forgive. Otherwise we give the enemy of our souls a foothold—a position from which to launch a full-scale attack on our hearts and minds, wreaking havoc and causing catastrophic damage.

Don't take a bath in wrath. Be cleansed by the Holy Spirit. Make things right. Forgive and be forgiven. "If it is possible, as far as it depends on you, live at peace with everyone" (Romans 12:18).

REFLECT

Are you angry with someone right now? If so, what can you do to resolve the situation?

Can you choose to forgive and let it go? Or is it something that needs to be confronted, confessed, or addressed?

PRAY

Lord, in my anger, don't let me sin. Don't let me do or say things I will regret—things that will cause harm to myself or others and dishonor You. Help me to keep short accounts, to be quick to apologize, quick to forgive, and eager to resolve disagreements and reconcile my relationships. I don't want to give the enemy a foothold in my heart and life. Teach me to be kind, loving, and merciful, just like You.

ME AND MY BIG **MOUTH**

> ❝ *Do not let any unwholesome talk come out of your mouths, but only what is helpful for building others up according to their needs, that it may benefit those who listen.* ❞

—Ephesians 4:29

You've probably heard the expression: "If you don't have anything nice to say, don't say anything at all." There's a lot of wisdom in that. But "nice" may not be the right adjective. After all, "nice" can be interpreted to mean pleasant or happy, avoiding anything serious or difficult, keeping things surface and shallow and polite—if insincere.

Sometimes the best words we can speak are strong words, bold words, words that are honest and direct. These kinds of words may be challenging, inspiring, encouraging. They may be informative or educational. They may be convicting, even painful, if they cause us or those around us to confront wrong thinking or wrongdoing, sin, selfishness, or pride.

The Bible teaches, "Faithful are the wounds of a friend" (Proverbs 27:6 ESV).

So the real question is not whether our words are "nice" but whether they are helpful. Do they ultimately strengthen and build up those who hear? Do our words empower others to be all that God meant for them to be?

Or do our words tear others down, judge them, criticize or belittle them? Do our words stir up gossip, anger, and strife? Do they cause needless controversy or dissension?

James reminds us:

> The tongue is a small part of the body, but it makes great boasts. Consider what a great forest is set on fire by a small spark. The tongue also is a fire, a world of evil among the parts of the body. It corrupts the whole person, sets the whole course of one's life on fire, and is itself set on fire by hell. (James 3:5–6)

Jesus said that our words begin in our hearts, that out of the overflow or abundance of our hearts, our mouths speak (Luke 6:45). If we want to change the words we speak, we first need His help to change our hearts. We need the Holy Spirit to show us the thoughts and attitudes that need reforming or reframing. We need to spend time filling our hearts with the truths of His Word, so that His truths are what come spilling out of us.

Then we can be sure we will always have something "nice"—something helpful, something beneficial—to say!

REFLECT

Imagine you are the star of your own reality TV show. If camera crews were following you around 24/7, if your words were broadcast nationwide, would you be thankful for the opportunity to be Christ's witness—or would you have reason to be embarrassed or ashamed?

PRAY

Lord, don't let any unwholesome talk—any vulgar, crude, cruel, critical, or complaining words—come out of my mouth today. Set a guard over my lips, so that nothing evil escapes them. Remind me throughout the day to speak only words that are helpful to others—words that build up, not tear down. Words that inspire and encourage and uplift those who hear them. May my words always be a blessing and a benefit to others. In Jesus' name, amen.

MERCY **ME**

> " *Get rid of all bitterness, rage and anger, brawling and slander, along with every form of malice. Be kind and compassionate to one another, forgiving each other, just as in Christ God forgave you.* "

—Ephesians 4:31–32

Jesus once told a story about a king who decided to bring his accounts up-to-date with servants who had borrowed money from him. One of his debtors was brought before him—a man who owed him millions of dollars. There was no way that the man could pay, so the king ordered that all of his possessions and property be sold and put toward the debt. Furthermore, the man himself should be sold as a slave, along with his wife and children—as part of the payment.

"But the man fell down before his master and begged him, 'Please, be patient with me, and I will pay it all.' Then his master was filled with pity for him, and he released him and forgave his debt" (Matthew 18:26–27 NLT).

Notice that the master didn't give him more time or reduce his debt, but he *forgave* it. He released the debtor from the burden, the obligation, the responsibility—completely. Imagine how that man must have felt! How his wife and children felt! The relief. The joy. The gratitude.

But then something even more shocking happened. The man whose debt had been forgiven had barely left the king's court when he ran into a fellow servant who owed him a few thousand dollars.

> He grabbed him by the throat and demanded instant payment. His fellow servant fell down before him and begged for a little more time. "Be patient with me, and I will pay it," he pleaded. But his creditor wouldn't wait. He had the man arrested and put in prison until the debt could be paid in full. (Matthew 18:28–30 NLT)

The merciful king soon heard about the incident. He sent for the debtor he had forgiven and said,

> "You evil servant! I forgave you that tremendous debt because you pleaded with me. Shouldn't you have mercy on your fellow servant, just as I had mercy on you?" Then the angry king sent the man to prison to be tortured until he had paid his entire debt. (Matthew 18: 32–34 NLT)

In case anyone somehow missed the point of this story, Jesus added, "That's what my heavenly Father will do to you if you refuse to forgive your brothers and sisters from your heart" (Matthew 18:35 NLT).

If we don't want God to hold our sin against us, then we must not hold others' sins against them. God has forgiven us; He requires that we forgive others. We may rationalize that our sins are smaller in comparison . . . that what someone else has done to us is far worse than anything we ourselves have done. But we don't know that. And in any case, we are not the judge—God is. It is His responsibility to deal with them and their sin.

"Do not take revenge, my dear friends, but leave room for God's wrath, for it is written: 'It is mine to avenge; I will repay,' says the Lord" (Romans 12:19).

Choose to release the hurt, the anger, the bitterness—the desire to be avenged or exonerated. Leave it (and the person who hurt you) in God's hands. Forgive just as Christ forgave you.

REFLECT

Is there someone who has sinned against you—someone you need to forgive today?

PRAY

Father, help me to get rid of any bitterness, rage, anger, or malice in my heart. I don't want to slander others or fight with them or cause harm to come to them. I want to be kind and compassionate, merciful and tenderhearted toward others. I know that I myself am a deeply flawed, frail human being—a sinner in desperate need of a Savior. I have made many mistakes. I have been selfish, thoughtless, even reckless. I have been stubborn, prideful, and rebellious. I have accidentally hurt other people. I've even deliberately hurt other people. I so desperately need Your mercy, forgiveness, and grace. Teach me to extend this same mercy, this same forgiveness, this same grace to others.

A SWEET **FRAGRANCE**

> " *Follow God's example, therefore, as dearly loved children and walk in the way of love, just as Christ loved us and gave himself up for us as a fragrant offering and sacrifice to God.* "

—Ephesians 5:1–2

D o you know how perfume is made? Designing a new fragrance is a complicated process involving a combination of various oils, herbs, spices, and, of course, flowers. To make the most of a flower's fragrance, you have to crush it. When the petals are crushed, broken open, and pulled apart, that's when the truest, richest, deepest fragrance spills out.

You know, God is creating you to be a one-of-a-kind Designer fragrance. He has brought all the ingredients together, orchestrated all the details of your life—causing some and allowing others—to bring out the best in you, to help you live strong, and to fulfill His purposes for you. As you surrender to the process, you become more and more like Jesus. You bring glory to Him—and you bring others to Him.

> Everywhere we go, people breathe in the exquisite fragrance. Because of Christ, we give off a sweet scent rising to God, which is recognized by those on the way of salvation—an aroma redolent with life. (2 Corinthians 2:14–15 MSG)

In other words, to God and to others, we smell like Jesus! Or at least we're supposed to. We can inspire, challenge, comfort, soothe, and strengthen others by bearing the beautiful fragrance of Christ to a world lost in sin. Others smell something rare, something precious, something wonderful—and it draws them to Him!

By nature, the process requires crushing. The Bible tells us that Jesus Himself was crushed and broken on our behalf. He became a pleasing aroma when He bore our sins—when He suffered and died on the cross, taking the punishment in our place. He gave off the fragrance of obedience, submission, and devotion to the will of God.

Was it worth it—all that suffering—to become the source of eternal salvation for all who believe? Jesus thought it was. "For the joy set before him he endured the cross, scorning its shame" (Hebrews 12:2). Jesus had His eyes on eternity. And so should we.

As God's grace reaches more and more people, there will be great thanksgiving, and God will receive more and more glory. That is why we never give up. Though our bodies are dying, our spirits are being renewed every day. For our present troubles are small and won't last very long. Yet they produce for us a glory that vastly outweighs them and will last forever! (2 Corinthians 4:15–17 NLT)

Over and over God reminds us that our suffering has a greater purpose. He promises that it is not for nothing. "In all things God works for the good of those who love him" (Romans 8:28). One day we will see. We will understand. And we won't regret a single step of the process He used to make us a beautiful aroma, a sweet-smelling fragrance that brings pleasure and glory and honor to Him!

REFLECT

What fragrance are you giving off today?

Can others "smell" Jesus in you?

PRAY

God, fill me with Your love today and help me to live a life of love—a life of obedience, a life of devotion, a life of sacrifice. Jesus, You gave Your life for me. I want to live my life for You. I offer You all that I am, all that I have, all that I hope to be. I surrender myself completely to You. May everything about my life—all that I say and do—be an expression of my love for You. May others be drawn by the sweet fragrance, the pleasing aroma, and give their hearts and lives to You.

A SHINING **LIGHT**

" *For you were once darkness, but now you are light in the Lord. Live as children of light (for the fruit of the light consists in all goodness, righteousness and truth) and find out what pleases the Lord.* "

—Ephesians 5:8–10

There's a story about a woman who got pulled over for what she thought was a routine traffic stop, only to find herself suddenly facedown in the gravel, with her hands cuffed behind her back.

A few minutes later, the arresting officer apologized profusely as he sat the stunned woman upright and removed the handcuffs.

"Ma'am," he said, "I'm so sorry. But I've been following you for about three miles now. Time after time, I watched you lay on the horn and tailgate the people in front of you who were driving too slow. You slammed your fist on the dashboard when you missed the last light. When I pulled up behind you I could hear you swearing and making obscene gestures at the guy who accidentally cut you off. I saw the fish on the bumper sticker and the cross hanging from the rearview mirror, and I assumed the car must be stolen!"

Ouch! As Christians, we have to ask ourselves, what kind of example are we setting? What kind of witness are we giving? Philippians 1:27 reminds us, "Whatever happens, conduct yourselves in a manner worthy of the gospel of Christ."

It's not just our own reputation on the line, or even that of our brothers and sisters in Christ. It's God's reputation at stake. As His children, we are a reflection of Him.

Knowing Jesus is supposed to make a noticeable difference in the way we live. Those around us should see it and be drawn to it. It's why we're called to be children of light, to live a life of light in a dark and dying world!

Learning to live a life of light does take time. It takes the work of the Holy Spirit in us and through us. And yes, it takes effort on our part to learn to discern what is and is not pleasing to the Lord. What things to hold on to and what things to leave behind. But we have the Word of God to help us. And we have an amazing teacher called grace:

For the grace of God has appeared that offers salvation to all people. It teaches us to say "No" to ungodliness and worldly passions, and to live self-controlled, upright and godly lives in this present age, while we wait for the

blessed hope—the appearing of the glory of our great
God and Savior, Jesus Christ. (Titus 2:11–13)

He'll be here soon. Let's do our best to be a good reflection
and make Him proud.

REFLECT

Does the light of Jesus shine through you in your church
and in your community? Does it shine in your workplace or
school? Does it shine in your home?

PRAY

*Jesus, You are the Light of the World. Shine Your light in me today.
Chase away the darkness of sin, the darkness of fear and doubt and
despair. Fill me with the light of Your truth, Your Word. Produce in me
the fruit of righteousness—the evidence that Your Holy Spirit lives in me
and works in me and works through me. Teach me what is pleasing to
You. Make me a shining example of Your amazing grace, redeeming love,
and life-changing power. May others be drawn to You through me.*

THE TIME WE'VE **BEEN GIVEN**

> 66 *Be very careful, then, how you live—not as unwise but as wise, making the most of every opportunity, because the days are evil.* 99

—Ephesians 5:15–16

In J. R. R. Tolkien's classic Lord of the Rings trilogy, a young hobbit named Frodo sets out on a perilous quest to destroy a ring of power that threatens to devastate Middle Earth. In one scene Frodo expresses great frustration and discouragement. The lines have been drawn for the ultimate battle of good and evil. And the good are terribly outnumbered. The growing darkness—the corruption of what was once good and true—is oppressive. The quest seems hopeless.

"I wish the ring had never come to me," Frodo exclaims. "I wish none of this had ever happened." His friend Gandalf replies, "So do all who live to see such times, but that is not for them to decide. All we have to decide is what to do with the time that is given to us."[8]

Reading through the letters to the early church in the New Testament, we can tell that many of those first disciples felt the same discouragement as Frodo. Hard-pressed on every side, persecuted, suffering—they struggled to hold on to hope in the face of overwhelming evil. But the apostles reminded them of the ultimate victory that was theirs in Christ and challenged them in the meantime to stand fast, to fight the good fight, and to make "the most of every opportunity, because the days are evil."

We, too, live in dark days. Wickedness seems to be flourishing. Monstrous evil goes unchecked. And immorality is so rampant, so commonplace, so ordinary that some of us are getting drawn into it without even realizing it. Our objections are ignored, and our defenses are torn—or worn—down. Our vulnerabilities are used against us. We're seduced. Before we know it, we are far, far from the life of purity, honesty, and integrity that God has called us to.

The Scripture tells us, "Be strong in the Lord and in his mighty power. Put on the full armor of God, so that you can take your stand against the devil's schemes" (Ephesians 6:10–11). Whatever you do, keep fighting! Offense and defense. For yourself, your family, your church, and community. For the kingdom of God. Win as many battles as you can.

Don't surrender to the darkness or become part of it. "Live holy and godly lives as you look forward to the day of God and speed its coming" (2 Peter 3:11–12).

Remember, these words were not just written for the early

church but for us as well. It's God's answer to our question: What shall we do with the time that is given to us?

REFLECT

How can you make the most of the time God has given you today—*this next twenty-four hours*—to honor and bring glory to Him?

PRAY

Father, teach me to be wise, to recognize the signs of the time in which I live, to be aware and alert to what You are doing in the world around me. Show me how Your will is unfolding and what part I may play, how Your plans and purposes can be accomplished.

Help me to make the most of every opportunity to grow deeper in my relationship with You, to live stronger in my stand against evil. Let me love faithfully and live purely. Let me lead others to You. May I wholeheartedly do my part to advance Your kingdom and Your will here on earth in the time You have given me. Amen.

WHERE THERE'S A **WILL**

" *Therefore do not be foolish, but understand what the Lord's will is.* **"**

—Ephesians 5:17

It's a common complaint of women everywhere: men are forever getting lost, because they usually won't stop and ask for directions. To be perfectly fair, it's an affliction that affects both genders. Women may be quick to buy a map for a road trip, but there are plenty of other projects they plunge into—only to find themselves in over their heads. And just like the guys, they often refuse to ask for help.

Why is that? Why are we all so reluctant to ask for guidance and direction when we need it? Maybe it's because we're in denial; we won't admit that we have a problem. Sometimes, we're embarrassed about it. We don't want anyone to think we're ignorant. Other times, we're so busy trying to solve things on our own that it doesn't occur to us to ask for help.

When you think about it, this is really silly. We just keep

taking one wrong turn after another, digging ourselves deeper into a pit, when the best solution is to ask for help. James 1:5 says, "If any of you lacks wisdom, you should ask God, who gives generously to all without finding fault."

God never says to us, "How many times do I have to help you? When are you going to figure it out on your own?" No—of course not! He loves to help us. He longs to help us.

When we earnestly, intently, purposely listen for God's direction, we receive it. "Whether you turn to the right or to the left, your ears will hear a voice behind you, saying, 'This is the way; walk in it'" (Isaiah 30:21).

God has already given us a lot of wisdom and direction in Scripture. He has already revealed so much about His will. We just need to read His Word. Walk in it. Put it into practice.

But even when we don't know what God's will is or how to apply the Scriptures to our specific circumstances, we're not lost and on our own. Help is only a prayer away.

God may slip a thought or an idea into our hearts. He may speak through His Word—directing us to specific passages, enlightening us as to their meaning and application. He may speak through circumstances or through the wise counsel of other believers. In countless ways, to those who are listening, He makes His voice heard.

Having trouble with your teenager? Ask God to show you what to do. Problems at work? Ask God. Need inspiration for a creative project? Ask God. Deciding whether to move or stay put, step out in faith or wait patiently for Him? Whatever situation you face today, God knows exactly what you should do. What He wants you to do. What is best for you. And He'll show you—if you just ask Him!

REFLECT

What can you say is God's will for you right now, in this moment—this season of your life? In what area do you need His wisdom and direction?

PRAY

Lord, open my heart and mind to Your truth. Fill me with the wisdom of Your Word and Your Holy Spirit. Teach me to hear Your voice, to know and understand what Your will is—for me, for my family, for my church and community. Help me to fulfill Your plans and purposes for me, for Your glory and my good.

LOVE **SONG**

> ❝ *Be filled with the Spirit, speaking to one another with psalms, hymns, and songs from the Spirit. Sing and make music from your heart to the Lord.* ❞

—Ephesians 5:18–19

When we see God move in our midst, when we catch just a glimpse of who He is and what He has done for us, it's only natural to respond in awe and gratitude, with words of praise and worship and thanksgiving. And not just in the face of the extraordinary, the supernatural, and miraculous, but in the "ordinary" everyday miracles, the beauty and majesty of creation itself. As nineteenth-century poet Elizabeth Barrett Browning put it, "Earth's crammed with heaven, and every common bush afire with God."[9]

The Westminster Catechism asks the question: What is the chief and highest end of man?[10] Scripture tells us our answer: to glorify God and to enjoy Him forever. Nothing brings us more fulfillment than to worship Him—to do that which we were created to do: "Worship the LORD in the splendor of his holiness" (Psalm 29:2 NLT).

God deserves our worship, and it's not arrogant or vain or needy of Him to ask for it. He created us so that He could share Himself with us. He wants us to enjoy all that He is and all that He gives, so we can revel in His beauty, in His majesty, in His holiness—and respond in heartfelt worship.

If you've ever done something kind or thoughtful or loving or selfless—if you've ever created something beautiful or meaningful—you know how special it is to share it with someone else. In essence, you are giving them the gift of yourself. And if the other person recognizes your thoughtfulness, your effort, your sacrifice—and they have an appreciation for you as the giver—then there's something very special about their expression of thanks. In that moment it blesses you as it blesses them. It brings the two of you closer. And you have just a tiny taste of what the worship of God is all about, why it's so meaningful to God and to us.

In one sense, all of our lives are meant to be worship—everything we are, everything we do, everything we say. But there's something special about the way we express our hearts in song: with words that express our admiration, our appreciation, our adoration of God. Whether written or spoken or sung, these words have incredible power—not only to glorify God and bless His heart, but to bless our hearts. They inspire us, uplift us, renew us, and refresh us.

The words we speak we believe. When our words express our hope in Christ, our faith and trust in Him—when we confess that "God is good, all the time"—our hearts and minds receive it and believe it. Whether these words are expressed in corporate worship, in our personal quiet time, in a small group Bible study, or over coffee with a friend, they have the same effect: they build up our spirits, and through us, the spirits of those around us. This is one reason Ephesians 5:19 urges us to speak "to one another with psalms, hymns, and songs from the Spirit. Sing and make music from your heart to the Lord."

So take some time today to make a joyful noise—let your heart sing to God—and encourage someone else to sing along!

REFLECT

If your life was a love song to Jesus, what would the title be?

PRAY

*Lord Jesus, fill me with Your Spirit. Fill my lips with Your praise—
with psalms and hymns and songs from the Spirit that will bless my
brothers and sisters in Christ and encourage them to worship You.
Let my whole life be a love song to You, and let me always sing
and make music in my heart to You.*

SONGS IN THE **NIGHT**

> " *. . . always giving thanks to God the Father for everything, in the name of our Lord Jesus Christ.* "

—Ephesians 5:20

When life throws you a curve ball—when something happens that knocks you for a loop—how do you respond? What about when you're falsely accused, unjustly attacked, persecuted for taking a stand?

It's tempting at these times to curl up and cry a river of tears, throw ourselves a pity party, or surrender to the feeling that we've been abandoned or forsaken by God. But that's not how Paul and Silas responded. Just for preaching the gospel, these two men were severely beaten and thrown into prison, their feet put in the stocks. It would have been perfectly understandable if they'd given in to discouragement and despair—if they'd laid there moaning in pain or crying out to God in anguish.

But they didn't. The Bible tells us that at midnight, Paul and Silas were praying and worshiping and praising God, singing hymns from their heart to His. They were thanking Him for His goodness, mercy, and love. Thanking Him. In prison.

God sent an earthquake to shake the prison walls, setting Paul and Silas free. Because of their testimony in the midst of suffering and persecution, the jailor and his household were saved (Acts 16:25–34).

Sometimes the most powerful praise comes from the darkest of times.

Few of us will ever be tortured and imprisoned like Paul and Silas—but all of us have "dark nights of the soul"—times when discouragement and despair threaten to overwhelm us. Moments when we wonder what's going on and who's in control and how we will survive. But no matter how difficult the battle, we are more than conquerors through Him who loved us. "Neither death nor life, neither angels nor demons, neither our fears for today nor our worries about tomorrow—not even the powers of hell can separate us from God's love" (Romans 8:38 NLT).

The victory has been won. It's already ours. So even in our most difficult situations—in the dark nights of the soul—we have every reason to rejoice. Every reason to trust. Every reason to give thanks, regardless of our circumstances. "We know that in all things God works for the good of those who love him" (Romans 8:28).

Let us remember the example of our brothers in Acts 16. If we offer up a sacrifice of praise, if we give thanks in all things, then our eyes will be lifted from the misery of our circumstances to the beauty of our heavenly Father's face. We will find comfort and strength—and be a light to others, with our songs in the night.

REFLECT

What are you thankful for today?

Will you choose to thank God even for those things—those people, those circumstances—that you wouldn't normally count as "blessings"?

PRAY

Lord, I thank You for who You are and all that You have done for me. You have rescued me; You have saved me and redeemed me. I am Yours, now and forever. Thank You for the many blessings I take for granted . . . evidence of Your mercy and grace, Your love, Your protection and provision.

Thank You for the hardships, for the struggles, the pain. They have all taught me so much—are teaching me even now. And my trials have caused me, even forced me, to depend more fully on You. Be glorified in my life today. In the name of Jesus, I pray. Amen.

IT'S A GOOD **THING**

66 *Submit to one another out of reverence for Christ.* 99

—Ephesians 5:21

G od calls His precious children to submit to one another. Many of us hear the word *submit* and immediately conjure up negative images of weak, fearful, helpless beings (animals, people, countries) allowing their boundaries to be overrun, their rights to be trampled on. We see them passively, haplessly subjecting themselves to domination, and even evil or abuse at the will of a stronger, more aggressive entity.

But this is not the biblical definition of submission. The Greek word is actually a word that is often used in military scenarios: picture soldiers coming together under the leadership of other soldiers—officers, generals—to put into place an effective strategy, accomplish specific tasks, and march to victory in battle. Like the spiritual battles we face!

Biblical submission is a voluntary decision to relinquish "the right to be right" or first or in charge, no longer always insisting on having it your way. It means considering the needs of others, honoring and respecting their opinions, appreciating the unique talents and skills God has given them, and—in some cases—the leadership role, position, or responsibility He has appointed to them. At times, and in certain situations, we ourselves may be called to lead. But there are most certainly times in all of our lives when we need to be willing to let others take the lead. Let them shine. Let them stumble and fall and learn from their mistakes, if necessary . . . but always with a humble, gentle, supportive, and loving attitude. For the sake of the kingdom!

Here are our marching orders:

Dear friends, since God so loved us, we also ought to love one another. (1 John 4:11)

Accept one another, then, just as Christ accepted you, in order to bring praise to God. (Romans 15:7)

Encourage one another and build each other up.
(1 Thessalonians 5:11)

Finally, all of you should be of one mind. Sympathize with each other. Love each other as brothers and sisters. Be tenderhearted, and keep a humble attitude. Don't repay evil for evil. Don't retaliate with insults when people insult you. Instead, pay them back with a blessing. That is what God has called you to do, and he will bless you for it. (1 Peter 3:8–9 NLT)

God sees (even when others don't) what it takes for us to set aside our natural selfishness, self-focus, and self-absorption, and put the needs of others first. Not to earn their love and approval or meet some deep-seated emotional needs of our own, but to express Christ's love for them, want what's truly best for them, give sacrificially to them, and honor Him in the process.

REFLECT

Think about your own life, all your different roles, responsibilities, and relationships. In what areas do you need to put the biblical principle of submission into practice?

PRAY

Lord, help me to have a submissive spirit—a humble spirit, a gentle spirit, a loving spirit—toward my brothers and sisters in Christ. I want to show my reverence for You and my adoration of You by respecting and obeying Your commands. Show me my own heart, reveal my motives to me, the secret thoughts and attitudes. Help me to bring them all under Your authority and Your control, so that they may be honoring toward others and glorifying to You.

AS GOOD **AS IT GETS**

> **❝** *. . . Christ loved the church and gave himself up for her to make her holy, cleansing her by the washing with water through the word, and to present her to himself as a radiant church, without stain or wrinkle or any other blemish, but holy and blameless.* **❞**

—Ephesians 5:25–27

I s this life as good as it gets? Author Randy Alcorn says it is—if you're an unbeliever.[11] Think about it. For those who do not put their faith and trust in Jesus—those who refuse His salvation—this world is as close to heaven as they will ever get. This world full of war, poverty, famine, disease, hardship and heartache, and betrayal and disappointment is as much paradise as they will ever experience. It only goes downhill from here. . . all the way down into hell, eternal separation from God. Far away and far apart from anything that is good or true or kind or loving, anything pleasant or happy or beautiful. Anything creative or inspiring and uplifting.

The good news is that for those who do choose Jesus, those who do believe in Him and trust Him and love Him and serve Him, this world is as close to hell as we will ever get. This is the most hardship, the most difficulty, the most pain, and the most evil we will ever face. And it's over before we know it, gone in a flash. (Think how quickly the last few years have flown by!) From here, it only gets better. We will find ourselves in heaven—a place so beautiful it defies description. A hope so glorious, it's beyond our ability to comprehend. A love so precious that nothing in this world can compare. The book of Revelation says of heaven,

> Look! God's dwelling place is now among the people, and he will dwell with them. They will be his people, and God himself will be with them and be their God. "He will wipe every tear from their eyes. There will be no more death" or mourning or crying or pain, for the old order of things has passed away. . . . There will be no more night. (vv. 21:3–4; 22:5)

A paradise of perfection, full of love, joy, peace, beauty, kindness, and light. We'll have all kinds of things to do, places to go, people to see . . . but only exciting, rewarding, invigorating, fulfilling things.

There's so much to look forward to, not the least of which is our wedding day—our wedding feast—the Marriage Supper of the Lamb.

Throughout the Scriptures, the marriage relationship between a husband and a wife is used as an analogy of the kind of loving, committed relationship God longs to have with each of us individually and with humanity as a whole. He designed marriage for that very purpose. In the New Testament, the church—which is made up of individual believers—is often referred to collectively as "the bride of Christ." Jesus is pictured as the passionate Bridegroom who would do anything—even lay down His life—for His one true love. Us.

So do you think you can hold on until then? Can you get through whatever time you've got left—not only by making the most of this life, but by hanging on to the hope of heaven? Maybe even bring a few people along with you. Share your hope with them. Introduce them to Jesus, so that they, too, will find that this world is by no means as good as it gets.

REFLECT

What do you most look forward to in or about heaven?

PRAY

Thank You, Jesus, that You loved us, Your church, and gave Yourself up for us to make Your church holy, cleansing us by the washing with water through the Word. We look forward to that day when You will present us to Yourself as a radiant church, without stain or wrinkle or any other blemish, but holy and blameless before You.
We are eager to see You face-to-face and celebrate our wedding day!

HONOR AND **OBEY**

> 66 *Children, obey your parents in the Lord,*
> *for this is right. 'Honor your father and mother'—*
> *which is the first commandment with a promise —*
> *'so that it may go well with you and that you*
> *may enjoy long life on the earth.'* 99

—Ephesians 6:1-3

H onoring our parents is one of the Ten Commandments: "Honor your father and your mother, so that
you may live long in the land the LORD your God is giving
you" (Exodus 20:12). This is the first commandment that
most children learn—the one they can most readily understand and apply to their own young lives. It's also the first
commandment to emphasize the blessings and rewards that
come with obedience.

When we're children, honoring our parents is as simple
as obeying them. Whether we like their rules, whether we
agree with them, or whether we want to obey—we respect

the authority God has given them and we obey. Learning to trust and obey our parents teaches us to trust and obey God.

But as adults, we are the heads of our own households. We have become the "parents"—the authority in the home. We are no longer obligated to live by our own parents' rules. We aren't required to submit to their authority. We answer directly to God for our choices, attitudes, and behaviors. So how do we apply this passage of Scripture?

As adults, honoring our parents means treating them with compassion, kindness, and respect. It may also mean looking out for their best interests, caring or providing for them—especially if they can no longer care or provide for themselves.

It sounds pretty simple. But truthfully, honoring our parents can be a challenge at any age and at any time, especially if our parents are less than perfect. (Let's face it: all of them are!) But what if our parents really—and I mean *really*—don't deserve it? What if they have been abusive, neglectful, willfully absent, or indifferent? What if they have mistreated us?

In Luke 6:27–28, 36, Jesus said, "Love your enemies, do good to those who hate you, bless those who curse you, pray for those who mistreat you. . . . Be merciful, just as your Father is merciful."

The harsh reality is that sometimes our enemies are members of our own families. God calls us to love them anyway. Forgive them, even if they don't ask us to. Treat them with courtesy and respect, regardless of whether they deserve it. Regardless of how they treat us.

By doing so, we're choosing to imitate our heavenly Father instead of our earthly parents. And we will receive from God His blessing and reward.

REFLECT

How, specifically, can you honor your parents—or the memory of your parents—today?

PRAY

Lord, show me how to do what is right and honor my father and my mother today, regardless of what kind of parents they are (or were). Help me to be patient and kind, tenderhearted, and forgiving toward them. I know how important it is to be obedient to Your Word in this matter, to respect those who have been or are now in authority over me. I want to honor and obey You, my heavenly Father, most of all.

As I honor my parents, may it go well with me—may I escape the
heartache that results from rebellion, the painful consequences
of disobedience, and may I enjoy every day You have
given me on this earth.

FATHER KNOWS **BEST**

66 Fathers, do not exasperate your children; instead, bring them up in the training and instruction of the Lord. 99

—Ephesians 6:4

Every one of us is a "child"—we all have parents we are to honor and respect. If we ourselves are parents, we also have the responsibility before God to love and nurture, teach and train, protect and provide for our children.

"Children, obey your parents in everything, for this pleases the Lord. Fathers, do not embitter your children, or they will become discouraged" (Colossians 3:20–21).

It's vitally important for children to learn to respect and obey their earthly father and mother, because this teaches them how to respect and obey their heavenly Father, God. But parents have responsibilities too. Paul tells parents not to embitter or exasperate—some translations say "aggravate," "irritate," or "provoke"—their children.

Parents provoke their children when they aren't clear about the rules and their consequences, and consistent in their enforcement. They aggravate their children when they make decisions that are arbitrary and unfair, and when they wield their power and authority like a sledgehammer. Hypocrisy breeds bitterness, disrespect, and even contempt. Broken promises. Absence or inattention. Abuse or neglect.

It's true that no earthly parent is perfect, but that's not an excuse for giving less than our best. It doesn't mean we shouldn't try harder to parent our kids "in the training and instruction of the Lord." When it comes to parenting, our own father and mother may or may not have set a good example for us. Ultimately our true role model is our heavenly Father. He is the perfect parent, always loving and kind, caring and compassionate. Trustworthy, faithful, and true. He is just. And He is merciful.

At times He disciplines us, just as all good fathers do. It's one of the ways a father shows his love—that he cares enough to take the time to teach his children right from wrong.

> We have all had human fathers who disciplined us . . . for a little while as they thought best; but God disciplines us for our good, that we may share in his holiness. No discipline seems pleasant at the time, but painful. Later on, however, it produces a harvest of righteousness and peace for those who have been trained by it. (Hebrews 12:9–11)

The point of discipline is not to put us in our place or to prove who's in charge, but to produce in us spiritual maturity, character, and integrity. Its purpose is to teach us, to challenge us, and to encourage us to develop our God-given potential—to become all that God meant for us to be.

This is something to keep in mind as we receive discipline—or administer it—today.

REFLECT

What is the difference between discipline and punishment?

Why does a loving Father discipline His children?

PRAY

God, You are the perfect Father! You are perfectly wise, just, loving, gracious, merciful, and kind. You never provoke or exasperate Your children. You never reject us or ignore us or abandon us.

Thank You for loving me enough to discipline me—to challenge me and encourage me, to teach and correct me. Help me to reflect Your true nature and follow Your perfect example. Show me how to nurture lovingly and guide wisely the children in my life and bring them up in the training and instruction of the Lord. In Jesus' name, amen.

WHO'S THE **BOSS?**

    Slaves, obey your earthly masters with respect and fear, and with sincerity of heart, just as you would obey Christ. Obey them not only to win their favor when their eye is on you, but as slaves of Christ, doing the will of God from your heart. Serve wholeheartedly, as if you were serving the Lord, not people, because you know that the Lord will reward each one for whatever good they do, whether they are slave or free. And masters, treat your slaves in the same way. Do not threaten them, since you know that he who is both their Master and yours is in heaven, and there is no favoritism with him.

—Ephesians 6:5–9

It's been estimated that when the apostle Paul wrote the book of Ephesians, there were more than sixty million slaves living in the Roman Empire. The Bible doesn't specifically forbid slavery; it was a common practice in almost every culture at the time. Some slaves were prisoners of war; others sold themselves or their family members into slavery for a period of time in order to pay off debts.

The Scripture does forbid kidnapping people and then making those kidnapped into slaves. The Bible also includes slave traders—those who sell other human beings without their consent—in a list of godless immoral people, such as liars, murderers, and adulterers (1 Timothy 1:9–11). According to Old Testament law, slaves were to be treated with dignity and respect. Provisions were made for them to earn or receive their freedom. In the New Testament, Paul made it clear that slaves and slave owners had equal standing in the kingdom of God—as brothers and sisters in Christ.[12]

There are principles in these passages of Scripture that we can apply today in the context of our relationships as employees and employers. For example, we should have a Christlike attitude toward our work and not participate in negative remarks or attitudes about our workplace.

Unfortunately, many of us feel taken advantage of by our employers—or our families. We're overworked, underpaid, and unappreciated. As our frustration grows, we become bitter and resentful. We complain to anyone who will listen, and we nurse our bad attitude. Our performance suffers, because we're having trouble finding the motivation to get out of bed, let alone give our best effort. And why should we? The ungrateful people we work for or work with don't deserve it, we think.

But as believers, we answer to a higher authority. We're called to a different standard. Paul writes,

> Whatever you do, work at it with all your heart, as working for the Lord, not for human masters, since you know that you will receive an inheritance from the Lord as a reward. It is the Lord Christ you are serving. (Colossians 3:23–24)

Maybe it's time for an attitude adjustment! Whatever your job may be, inside or outside the home, are you following the biblical directive to "work at it with all your heart"? Are you giving your best effort? Remember that as Christians, everything we do is an act of service to God. He is the one who will reward our efforts. Whether we're driving a truck or doing dishes, answering phones or processing paperwork: whatever we do, let's do our best to live strong and make our Boss proud!

REFLECT

If you really believed that your to-do list came from Jesus— that you were doing all these things for Him—how would it change the way you work?

How would it change your attitude about your work, the way you treat your coworkers, and the projects you face?

PRAY

Lord, help me to respect and obey those You have put in authority over me, just as I would obey You. Help me to give them my very best, not just to win their favor or approval—and not only when they're watching me—but at all times, as Your servant, doing Your will from my heart. Teach me to work at each task wholeheartedly, regardless of whether my efforts are appreciated or acknowledged. I know that ultimately my reward comes from You.

Likewise, help me to treat those under my authority the way I want to be treated, with kindness, dignity, and respect. You are their Master and mine—we, all of us, answer to You.

STAND YOUR **GROUND**

> *Finally, be strong in the Lord and in his mighty power. Put on the full armor of God, so that you can take your stand against the devil's schemes. For our struggle is not against flesh and blood, but against the rulers, against the authorities, against the powers of this dark world and against the spiritual forces of evil in the heavenly realms. Therefore put on the full armor of God, so that when the day of evil comes, you may be able to stand your ground, and after you have done everything, to stand.*

—Ephesians 6:10–13

The Bible tells us there is a battle raging all around us—a spiritual battle between the armies of God and the forces of darkness. Today's passage tells us that this unseen battle takes place in the "heavenly realms." And whether we realize it or not, we are a part of this battle. In fact, we're right in the middle of it. But not as helpless spectators or innocent bystanders. Each of us is a soldier for one side or the other. As the great apologist and theologian C. S. Lewis observed, "There is no neutral ground in the universe; every square inch, every split second, is claimed by God and counter-claimed by Satan."[13]

God calls us to take a stand for Him. To choose His Word, His will, His way. To answer the question, "Who is on the LORD's side?" (Exodus 32:26 KJV) with "Here am I" (Isaiah 6:8 KJV).

As God's soldiers, we're called to resist temptation, to refuse doubt and fear, to stay true under pressure, under attack, under persecution. We're not to wilt or crumple or collapse, but to stand firm in the strength He gives us—in the power that He supplies.

According to Bible scholar Francis Foulkes, "stand" is actually the key word in this passage: "The present picture is not of a march, or of an assault, but the holding of the fortress of the soul and of the Church for the Heavenly King."[14]

So we are standing not only for ourselves but for our friends and family, for our brothers and sisters in Christ, for God and His kingdom. And we are not alone. We are surrounded by others who are themselves taking a stand. Doing their part. We are surrounded by God's heavenly armies—His mighty warrior angels—and by God Himself.

And often, "standing" is all that He asks of us. He promises that He will do the rest.

"Do not be afraid or discouraged. . . . For the battle is not yours, but God's. . . . Take up your positions; stand firm and see the deliverance the LORD will give you" (2 Chronicles 20:15, 17).

REFLECT

Where is the battle being fought in your life today?

What can you do to take a stand?

PRAY

Lord, make me strong in You and Your mighty power today. I put on the full armor of God—the armor You have given me to equip me for battle—so that when I am under attack, I will be able to stand my ground and defend my position against the enemy.

My struggle is not against human enemies but against the powers of darkness, the spiritual forces of evil that wage war on my soul and in the world all around me.

In Your strength, in Your power, I know I can win the victory. Jesus, You have given me victory over sin and temptation, victory over the weakness of my flesh, victory over fear and doubt, victory over the devil and his evil schemes, victory over death and the grave. Today I take my stand in the power of the resurrected Christ, the Solid Rock. And I will not be moved.

DRESSED FOR **SUCCESS**

> ❝ *Stand firm then, with the belt of truth buckled around your waist, with the breastplate of righteousness in place, and with your feet fitted with the readiness that comes from the gospel of peace. In addition to all this, take up the shield of faith, with which you can extinguish all the flaming arrows of the evil one. Take the helmet of salvation and the sword of the Spirit, which is the word of God.* ❞

—Ephesians 6:14–17

Imagine you're at a hockey game. The anthem has been sung and the players are taking the ice. All of a sudden you notice something: the goalie isn't wearing his face mask. Or shin guards. Or padding. He doesn't have his stick or his skates.

Ridiculous, isn't it? No goalie in his right mind would guard the goal unprotected. Without his gear, a goalie is a sitting duck—defenseless against the onslaught of the opposing team. With players bearing down on him, and the puck flying full speed through the air, he could end up with life-threatening injuries. There's no question about it: if he's going to do his job right—and live to tell about it—a goalie's got to have his gear.

As Christians, we've also got to have our gear. The Bible tells us we face a brutal opponent—the enemy of our souls—and he's determined to take us out of the game (1 Peter 5:8). We, however, are not defenseless against Satan's attacks. We have been given heavenly gear to help us win the battle. In Ephesians 6:11, Paul describes it as the "full armor of God."

This armor includes the belt of truth, which holds everything together and keeps the rest of our soldier's uniform and armor in place. And the breastplate of righteousness is the protection of our hearts that comes from living with integrity and a clear conscience. Our feet are "fitted" or dressed, ready to go out and share the good news of the gospel. The shield of faith is a full-body shield covering us from head to toe, helping us stand strong and resist the attacks of the enemy. The helmet of salvation is our ultimate protection—we have been forgiven, saved, and redeemed by God. And we have a powerful weapon for both offense and defense: the sword of the Spirit, which is the Word of God. "Alive and active . . . it penetrates even to dividing soul and spirit, joints and marrow; it judges the thoughts and attitudes of the heart" (Hebrews 4:12).

Dressed daily in this spiritual armor, we are ready for battle. "Be on guard. Stand firm in the faith. Be courageous. Be strong" (1 Corinthians 16:13 NLT).

We can live strong, stand our ground, and win the victory!

REFLECT

Which piece of spiritual armor do you especially need to put on today?

PRAY

Today I'm putting on the full armor of God so that when I'm under attack, when I face trials or temptations, I will be able to stand my ground. I stand firm with the belt of truth around my waist, with the breastplate of righteousness guarding my heart, with my feet ready to take the gospel of peace wherever God sends me. I also take up the shield of faith with which I can extinguish all the flaming arrows of the evil one. On my head I place the helmet of salvation. I grab hold of the sword of the Spirit—the Word of God, sharp and true.

Lord, be with me in the heat of the battle and grant me victory I pray, in Jesus' mighty name.

THE CALL TO **PRAYER**

And pray in the Spirit on all occasions with all kinds of prayers and requests. With this in mind, be alert and always keep on praying for all the Lord's people.

—Ephesians 6:18

As Christians we are called to live a life of prayer and communion with God. It's with our prayers that we cry out to Him—we intercede for our friends and family, our community, and our country. In prayer, we express to God our hopes and dreams, our fears, our needs. We open our hearts to Him.

The amazing thing is that God never grows tired of listening to us. He doesn't get annoyed or irritated by the "interruption." He doesn't wish we'd stop pestering Him. He wants us to come to Him *more*. He wants us to come to Him first.

Here are just a few things the Scripture teaches us about prayer:

The earnest prayer of a righteous person has great power. (James 5:16 NLT)

Pray continually. (1 Thessalonians 5:17)

Do not be anxious about anything, but in every situation, by prayer and petition, with thanksgiving, present your requests to God. (Philippians 4:6)

Cast all your anxiety on him because he cares for you. (1 Peter 5:7)

Devote yourselves to prayer, being watchful and thankful. (Colossians 4:2)

And the Holy Spirit helps us in our weakness. For example, we don't know what God wants us to pray for. But the Holy Spirit prays for us with groanings that cannot be expressed in words. (Romans 8:26 NLT)

Prayer puts things into perspective. It keeps our focus on what matters most and helps us walk before God and others with humility. As the psalmist exclaimed, "My soul yearns, even faints, for the courts of the LORD; my heart and my flesh cry out for the living God" (Psalm 84:2).

In the movie *Shadowlands*, C. S. Lewis says to a friend, "I pray because I can't help myself. I pray because I'm helpless. I pray because the need flows out of me all the time—waking and sleeping. It doesn't change God—it changes me."

Lewis is right: prayer doesn't change God, in the sense that it doesn't make Him do something He doesn't already want or intend to do. However, Scripture indicates that prayer moves God to do things—and that without our prayers, He may not do them.[15] For reasons we may never fully understand, God chooses to use our prayers—chooses to respond to our prayers—as a means of achieving or accomplishing His purposes. He has given us the privilege and responsibility of partnering with Him in His work through the power of prayer.

Perhaps it's because the interaction between us and God is one of the ways He draws us closer, brings us into a deeper relationship with Him. By communicating with God (both talking and listening), we come to know Him better, understand and appreciate Him more. We learn to trust Him and more fully depend and rely on Him. It's what He longs for. And whether we realize it or not—it's what we long for too.

REFLECT

Which of the following expressions describes your typical approach to prayer: "When all else fails, pray" or "Before anything else, pray"?

PRAY

Father, teach me to pray in the Spirit—empowered by the Spirit, led by the Spirit, according to Your will, Your plans, and Your purposes. Help me to pray on all occasions, with all kinds of prayers and requests— in times of joy and celebration as well as in times of sorrow or desperation. For wisdom and guidance, for healing, for strength, for protection and provision, for peace. Through these prayers, draw me closer and closer to You.

Remind me to be alert and on guard, aware of the spiritual battle being fought all around me as I live strong for You. Help me to do my part, and to keep praying for my brothers and sisters in Christ as they fight their battles too! In Jesus' name, amen.

LIVING OUT **LOUD**

" Pray also for me, that whenever I speak, words may be given me so that I will fearlessly make known the mystery of the gospel, for which I am an ambassador in chains. Pray that I may declare it fearlessly, as I should. "

—Ephesians 6:19-20

Paul didn't ask the Ephesians to pray for his release from prison. He didn't ask them to pray for an official pardon or an unofficial, miraculous escape. He asked them to pray that he would have the courage to continue boldly proclaiming the gospel, regardless of what it cost him, right to the end. He just wanted God to give him the right words to say.

The psalmist had a similar prayer:

As for me, I will always have hope; I will praise you more and more. My mouth will tell of your righteous deeds, of your saving acts all day long—though I know not how to relate them all. I will come and proclaim your mighty acts, Sovereign LORD; I will proclaim your righteous deeds, yours alone. Since my youth, God, you have taught me, and to this day I declare your marvelous deeds. Even when I am old and gray, do not forsake me, my God, till I declare your power to the next generation, your mighty acts to all who are to come. (Psalm 71:14–18)

There is so much darkness in the world around us. So many lost and lonely. So many hopeless, hurting people. People who live desperate and defeated lives, even though the victory has been won.

"How can they call on him to save them unless they believe in him? And how can they believe in him if they have never heard about him? And how can they hear about him unless someone tells them?" (Romans 10:14 NLT).

How can *we* be silent? How can we fail to share the good news? Jesus is Victor. He has overcome. "Thanks be to God, who always leads us as captives in Christ's triumphal procession and uses us to spread the aroma of the knowledge of him everywhere" (2 Corinthians 2:14).

Sometimes it takes a little practice, a little preparation, a little thought about what God has given us to say, as well as when and where and how—and to whom—He might want us to say it. It's not a bad idea to memorize a few key scriptures, read a book, or take a class on evangelism.

But remember, we don't have to be highly educated or articulate or persuasive to share the gospel.

> Where is the wise person? Where is the teacher of the law? Where is the philosopher of this age? Has not God made foolish the wisdom of the world? . . . Brothers and sisters, think of what you were when you were called. Not many of you were wise by human standards; not many were influential; not many were of noble birth. But God chose the foolish things of the world to shame the wise; God chose the weak things of the world to shame the strong. (1 Corinthians 1:20, 26–27)

The Holy Spirit brings the conviction that leads to repentance. Jesus is the one who saves. What we can do is pray for wisdom and guidance, sensitivity, courage, boldness. Trust Him to give you the words to say. Let Him speak through you to reach someone else today.

REFLECT

What keeps you from sharing Jesus with the people you encounter each day?

PRAY

Lord Jesus, whenever I speak, give me the right words to say—words of love and kindness, words of wisdom and truth, words that lead others to put their faith in You. Help me to fearlessly and courageously make known the mystery of the gospel—the amazing story of Your redeeming love. Help me to declare it, proclaim it, shout it from the housetops . . . without fear of what others will think or say, without fear for my reputation or any suffering or persecution I may face. Your truth is greater. Your love is greater. Your salvation is greater than all of these things.

LOVE **ALWAYS**

❝ *Grace to all who love our Lord Jesus Christ with an undying love.* **❞**

—Ephesians 6:24

We've come to the end of our journey through the book of Ephesians. It's appropriate to pause and reflect on the truths we've explored, the prayers we've prayed, and the lessons we've learned along the way. But today let's look even further back . . . and consider our spiritual journey as a whole.

Do you remember what it was like when you first fell in love—truly in love—with Jesus? You were so excited to tell people about this new relationship! You couldn't spend enough time in His Word. You loved praying—talking to Him. You loved praising Him, worshiping Him, adoring Him. It seemed so easy to obey the Great Commandment: "Love the Lord your God with all your heart and with all your soul and with all your mind and with all your strength" (Mark 12:30).

Over time, however, many of us have found that our love can grow cold. Our passion can and does fade. One day we realize our relationship with Jesus just doesn't have that spark, the enthusiasm, the excitement it used to bring. Of course, it could be that we're going through a wilderness experience, a time of testing, when perseverance is paramount. Feelings can be deceiving—they're affected by so many different things and not the most reliable indicators of truth. Then again, maybe the truth is that our priorities have been gradually changing. Our focus shifting. Perhaps lately, we've been preoccupied with the dailiness of living. We've unintentionally neglected the most precious part of our life, our relationship with Christ.

In Revelation 2:4–5, Jesus Himself had one final message for the church in Ephesus. They had held on to the truth. They had persevered in suffering. But over time, they had lost their passion for Him: "You have forsaken the love you had at first. Consider how far you have fallen! Repent and do the things you did at first."

Don't make the same mistake as the Ephesians did. Don't let your love for the Lord grow cold. Instead, actively cultivate and nurture and deepen your love relationship with Jesus. Remember what God saved you from and how your life has changed. Think of how it would have been without Him. Relive some of the special experiences, the tender moments you shared— the divine appointments, miracles and answers to prayer. Did you used to sing along with your praise and worship albums all day long? Pull them out again. Or find some new ones! Did you never miss an opportunity to read the Word or spend time in fellowship with other believers? Make these things a priority once more. Did you used to share Jesus with everyone you met? Take time today to tell someone what God has done for you.

Before you know it, the spark will be back, the flame rekindled! Your love for Him will be an undying love. Just like His love for you.

He has chosen you for greatness—so live strong!

REFLECT

What one thing will you do today to express your love for Jesus?

PRAY

Lord Jesus, You have lavished Your love and life on me. I love You. Help me love You more and more. Test my love, strengthen my love, deepen my love, until it becomes an undying love. An all-consuming passion.
A magnificent obsession.

May Your grace and goodness and mercy surround me all the days of my life—until we meet face-to-face. How I long for that moment. I yearn for that day when we will be together forever. Come quickly, Lord Jesus. Amen.

NOTES

1. Oswald Chambers, *My Utmost for His Highest,* Updated Edition (Grand Rapids: Discovery House, 1992), December 8.

2. John Piper, *Spectacular Sins: And Their Global Purpose in the Glory of Christ* (Wheaton: Crossway Books, 2008).

3. See Hebrews 11:39–40 and Romans 4:9.

4. See Hebrews 12:1.

5. Christin Ditchfield, "The Narrow Path: Tino Wallenda-Zoppe's Highly Unusual Ministry," *Power for Living,* October 10, 1999.

6. Martha Bolton, *Reality Check: Sketches Focused on Being Real* (Kansas City: Lillenas Drama, 2000).

7. Patsy Clairmont, *Under His Wings* (Colorado Springs, CO: Focus on the Family, 1994), 108.

8. J. R .R. Tolkien, *The Fellowship of the Ring* (New York: Houghton Mifflin, 1994), 50.

9. Elizabeth Barrett Browning, *Aurora Leigh and Other Poems,* (New York: James Miller, 1864), 265.

10. "Westminster Larger Catechism," Center for Reformed Theology and Apologetics, accessed April 12, 2012, http://www.reformed.org/documents/index. html?mainframe=http://reformed.org/documents/larger1. html.

11. Randy Alcorn, *Heaven* (Carol Stream, IL: Tyndale, 2004), 28.

12. See Exodus 21:2–11; Leviticus 25:35–55; Deuteronomy 15:12–18; Galatians 3:28; Philemon 12–16; Ephesians 6:5–9.

13. C. S. Lewis, *Christian Reflections* (Grand Rapids: William B. Eerdmans, 1967), 33.

14. Francis Foulkes, *Ephesians* (Grand Rapids: William B. Eerdmans, 1989), 178.

15. See Ezekiel 22:30: "I looked for a man among them who would build up the wall and stand before me in the gap on behalf of the land so I would not have to destroy it, but I found none" (NIV 1984). Also see Jennifer Kennedy Dean's teaching in her book *Live a Praying Life!*, (Birmingham, AL: New Hope, 2010), 18–25.

ABOUT THE **AUTHOR**

Christin Ditchfield is an educator, author, conference speaker, and host of the syndicated radio program *Take It to Heart!* heard daily on hundreds of stations across the United States and around the world. Using real-life stories, rich word pictures, biblical illustrations, and touches of humor, Christin calls believers to seek after God enthusiastically, giving them practical tools to help deepen their personal relationship with Christ.

Christin has written dozens of best-selling gospel tracts and hundreds of columns, essays, and articles for national and international magazines such as *Focus on the Family*, *Today's Christian*, *Sports Spectrum*, and *Power for Living.* She is the author of more than sixty books, including *A Family Guide to Narnia*, *A Family Guide to the Bible*, *The Three Wise Women: A Christmas Reflection*, and *A Way with Words: What Women Should Know about the Power They Possess.*

A frequent guest on radio and television programs such as *Open Line*, *Midday Connection*, *Truth Talk Live*, *FamilyLife Today*, *Home-Word*, and Dr. D. James Kennedy's *Truths That Transform*, Christin holds a master's degree in biblical theology from Southwestern University.

For more information, visit www.TakeItToHeartRadio.com.

WORTHY
PUBLISHING

IF YOU LIKED THIS BOOK . . .

- Tell your friends by going to: www.prayingephesians.com and clicking "LIKE"

- Share the video book trailer by posting it on your Facebook page

- Log on to facebook.com/worthypublishing page, click "LIKE" and post a comment regarding what you enjoyed about the book

- Tweet "I recommend reading #prayingephesians by @Worthypub"

- Hashtag: #prayingephesians

- Subscribe to our newsletter by going to www.worthypublishing.com

WORTHY PUBLISHING
FACEBOOK PAGE

WORTHY PUBLISHING
WEBSITE